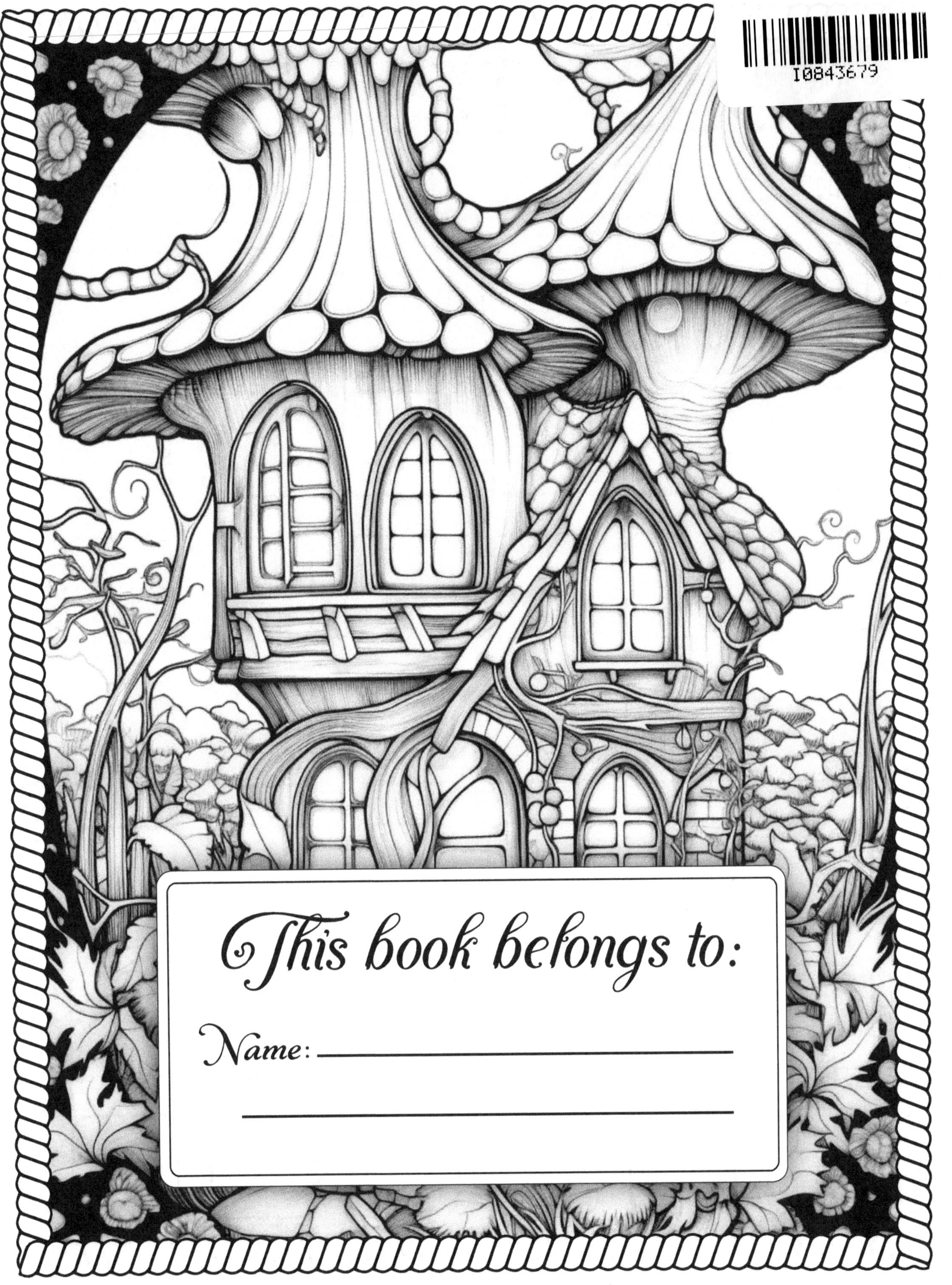
This book belongs to:
Name:

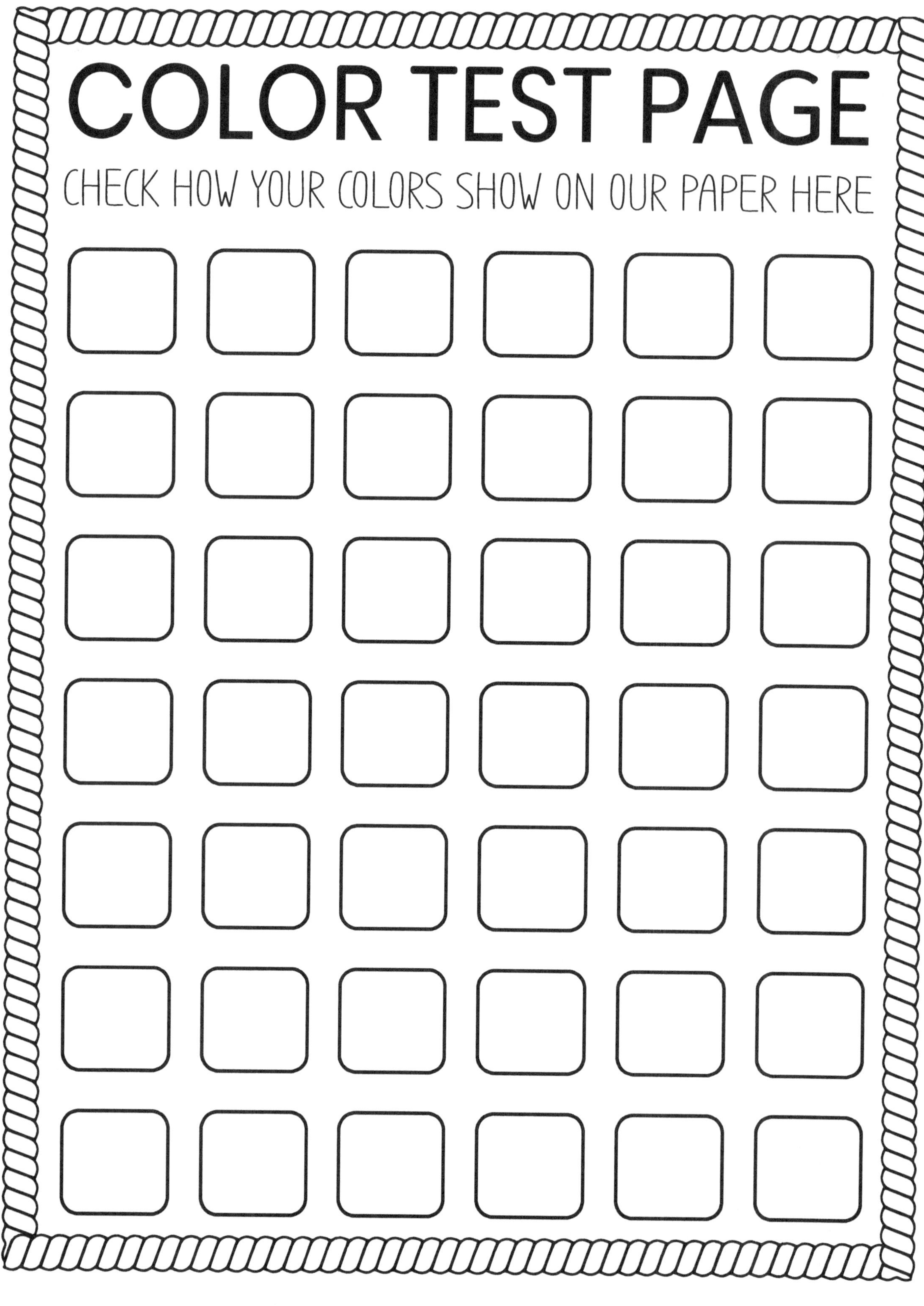

COLOR TEST PAGE
CHECK HOW YOUR COLORS SHOW ON OUR PAPER HERE

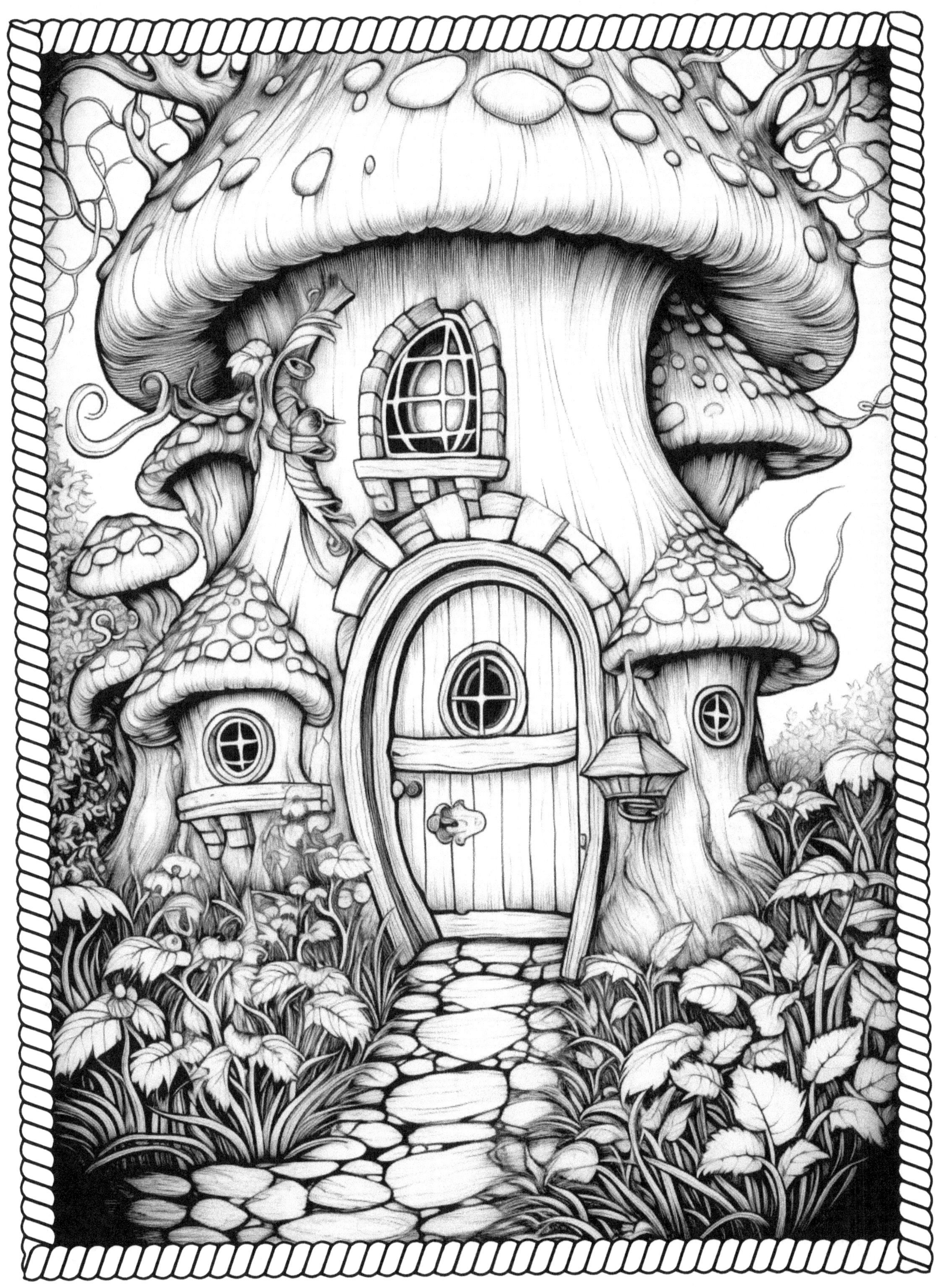

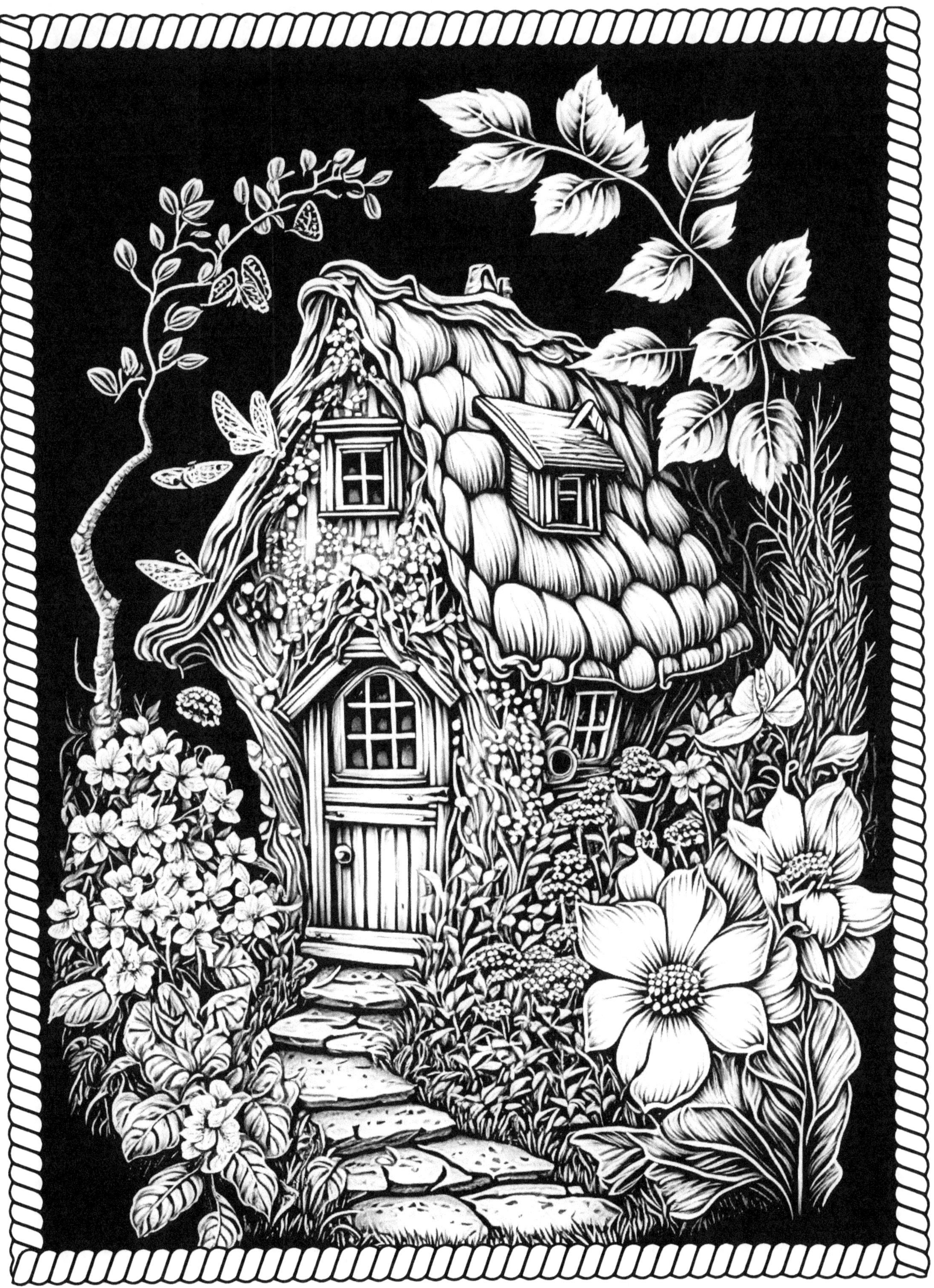

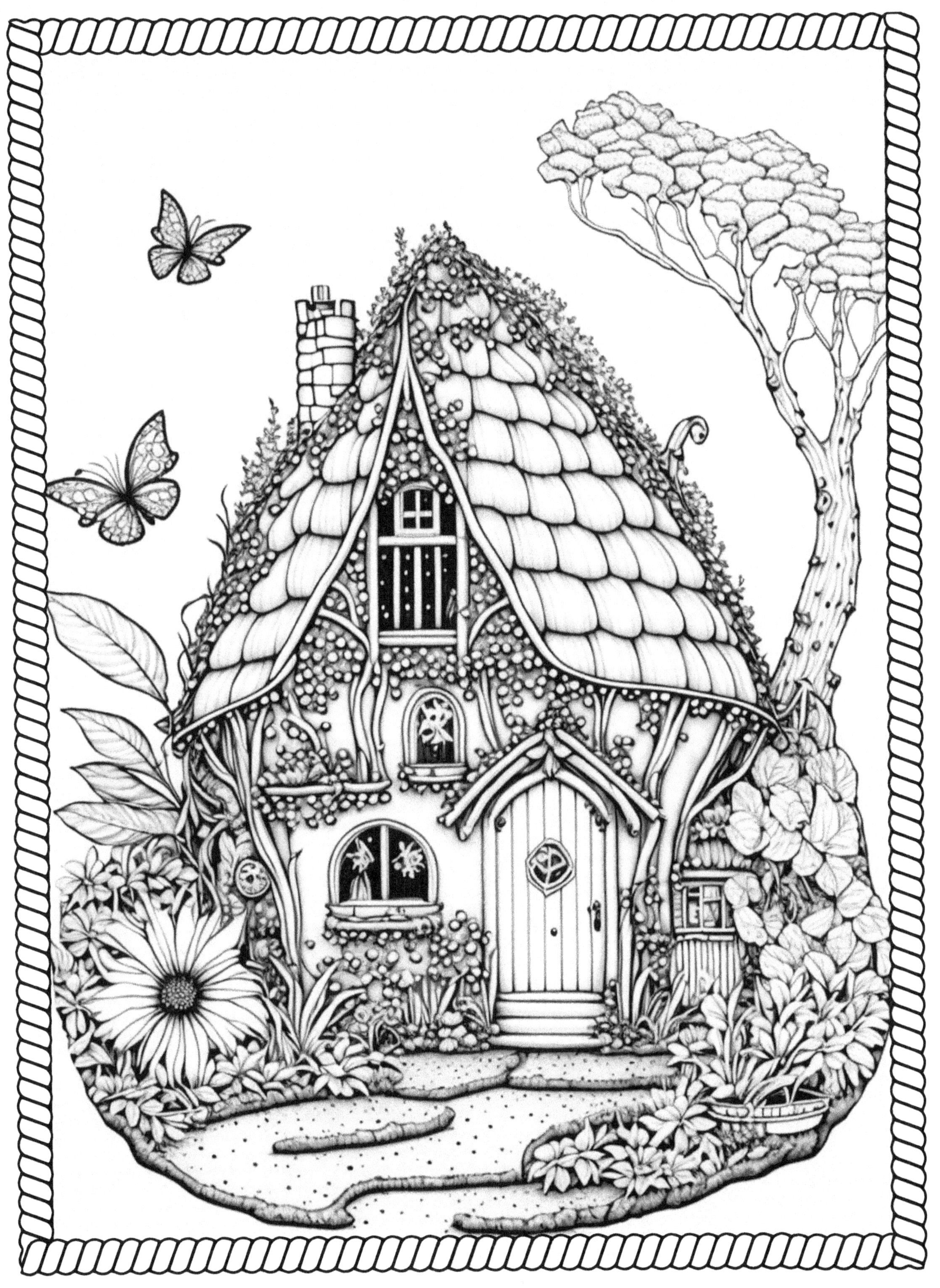

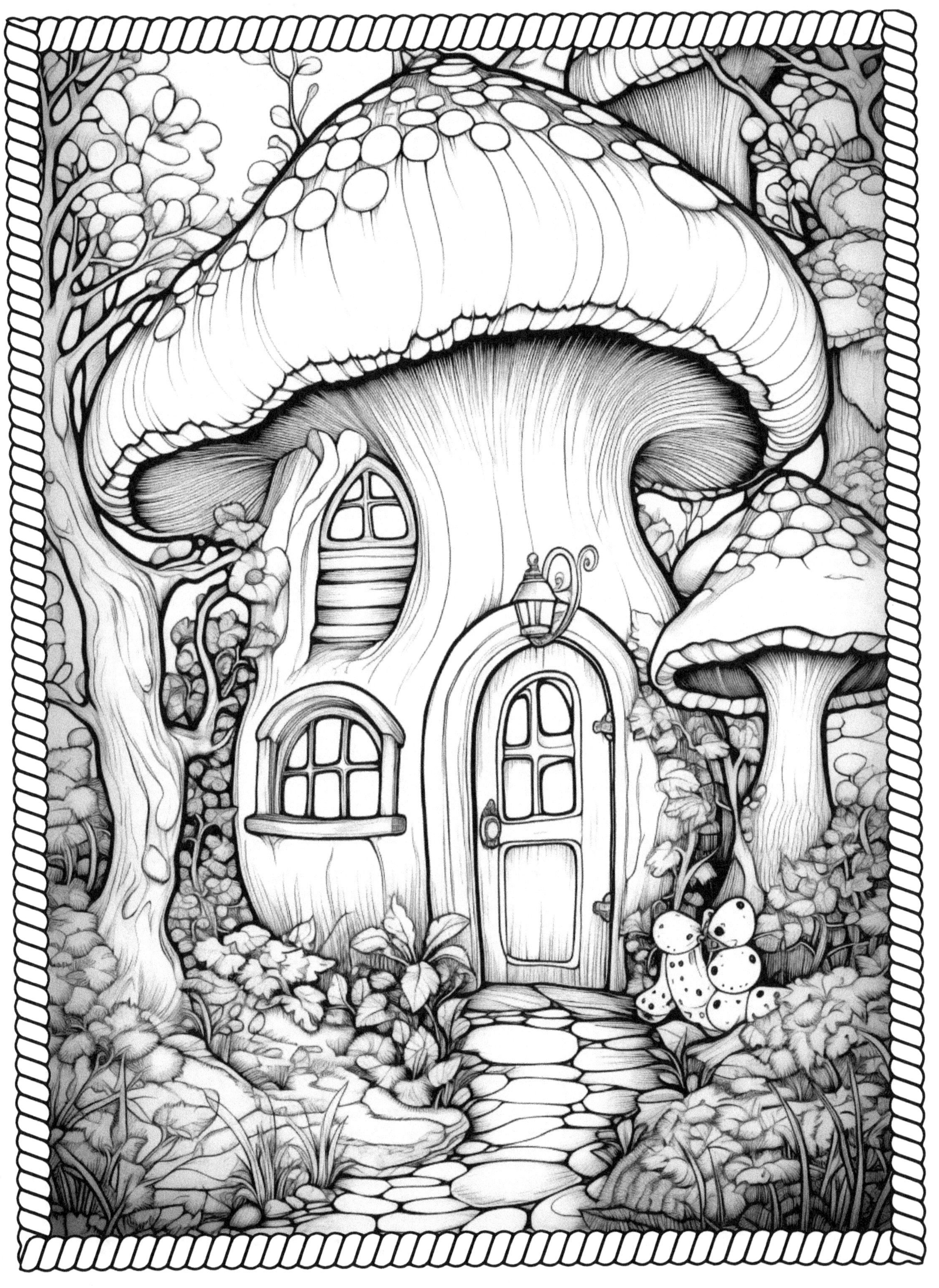

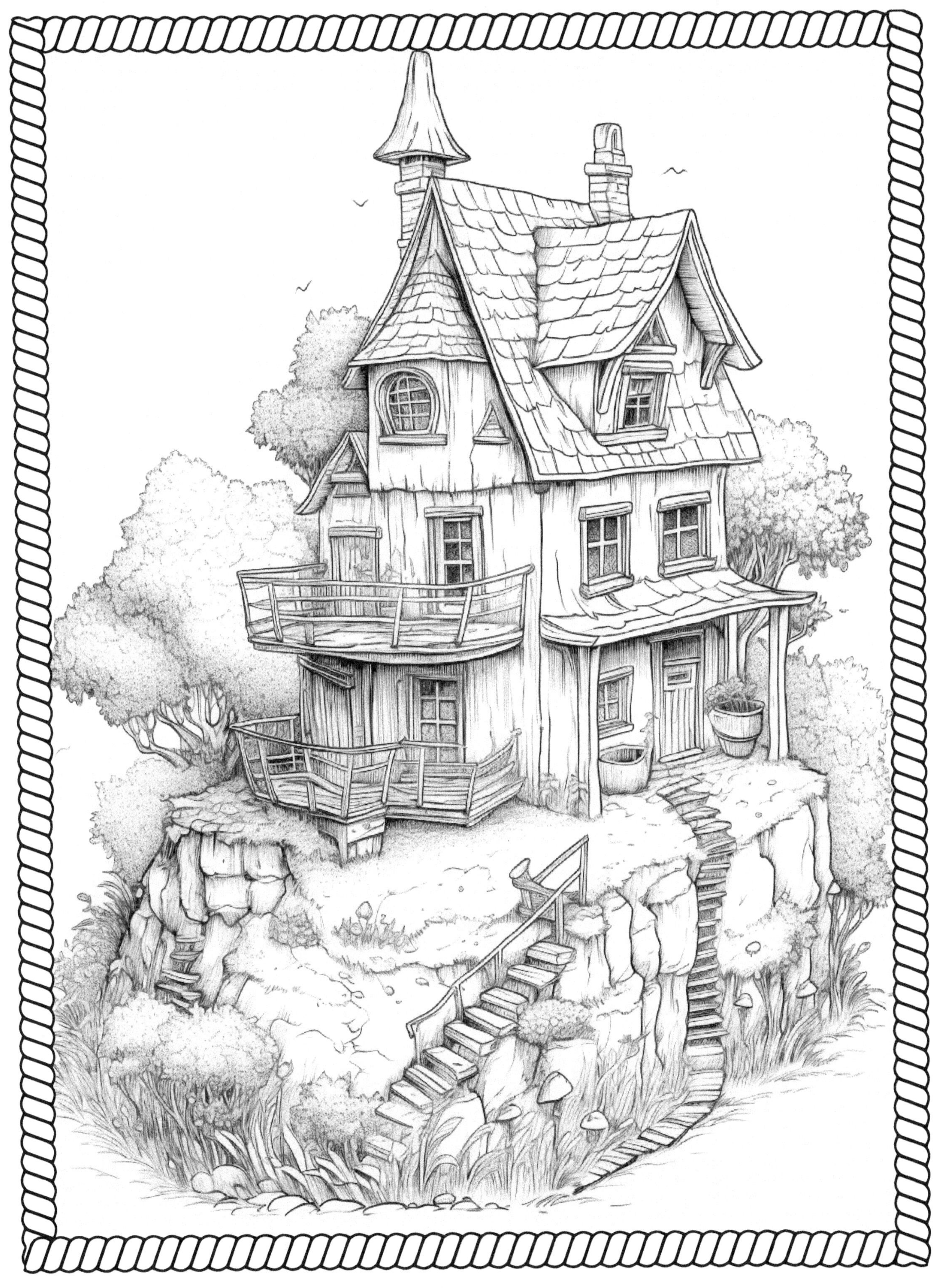

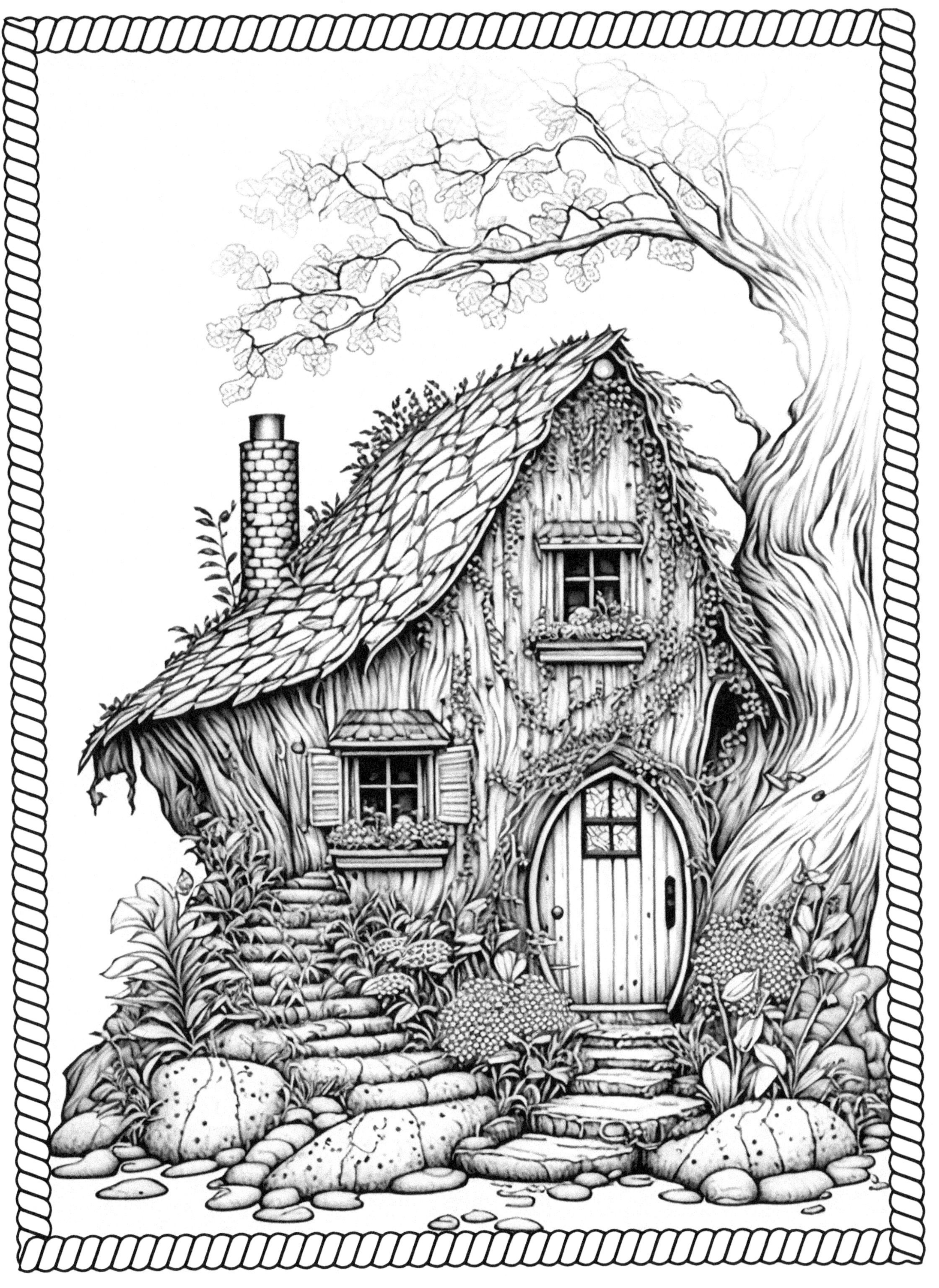

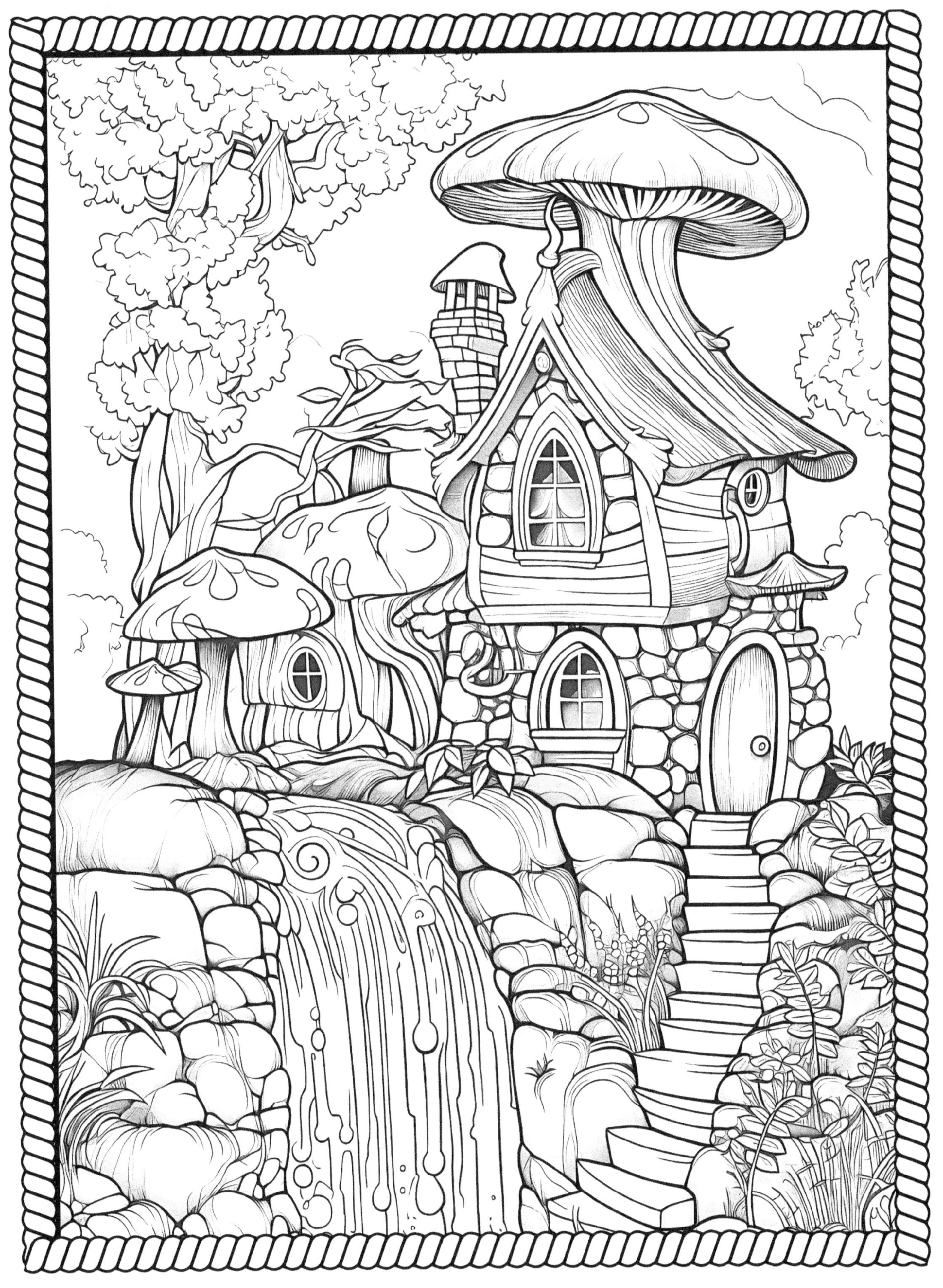

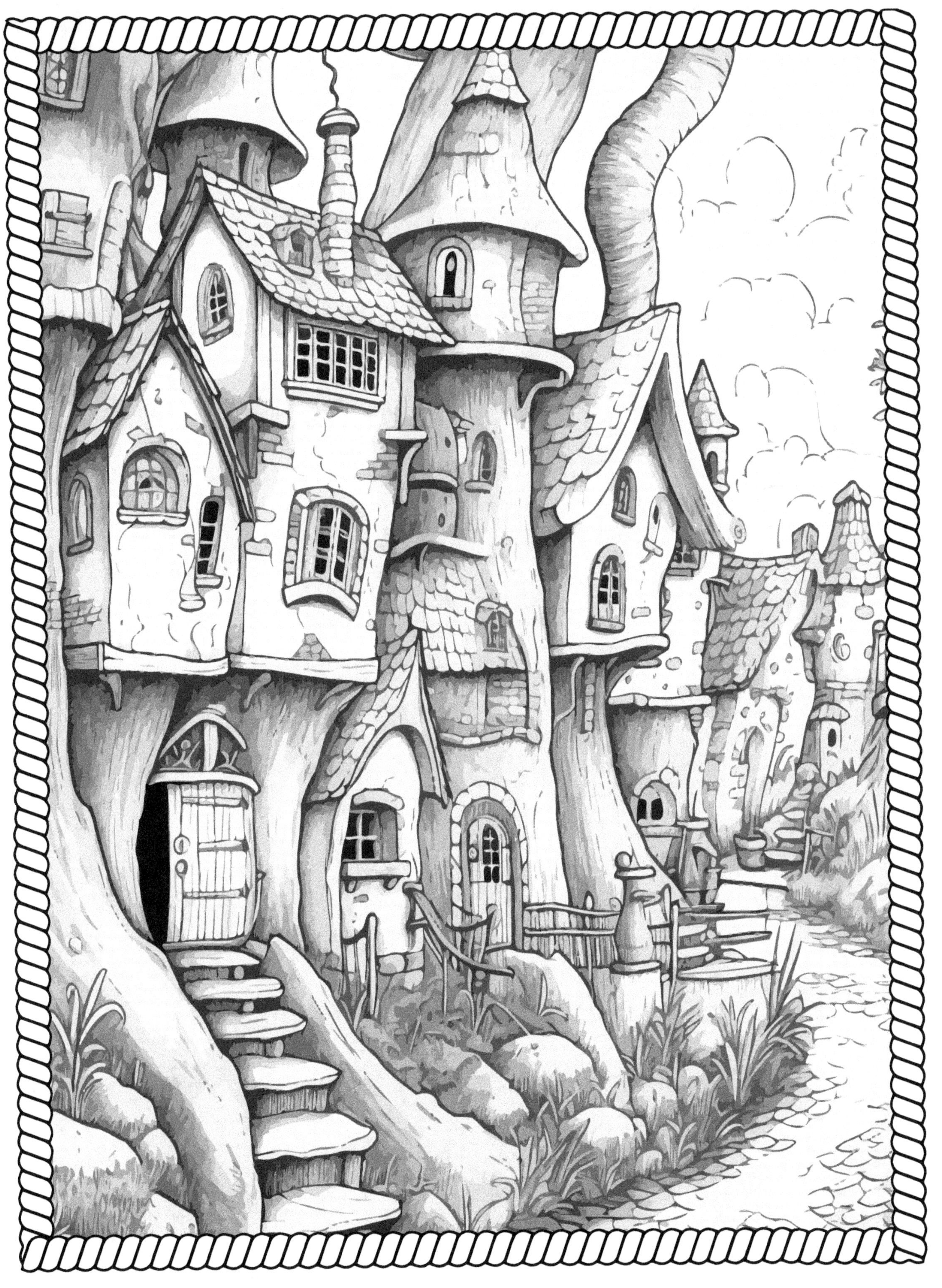

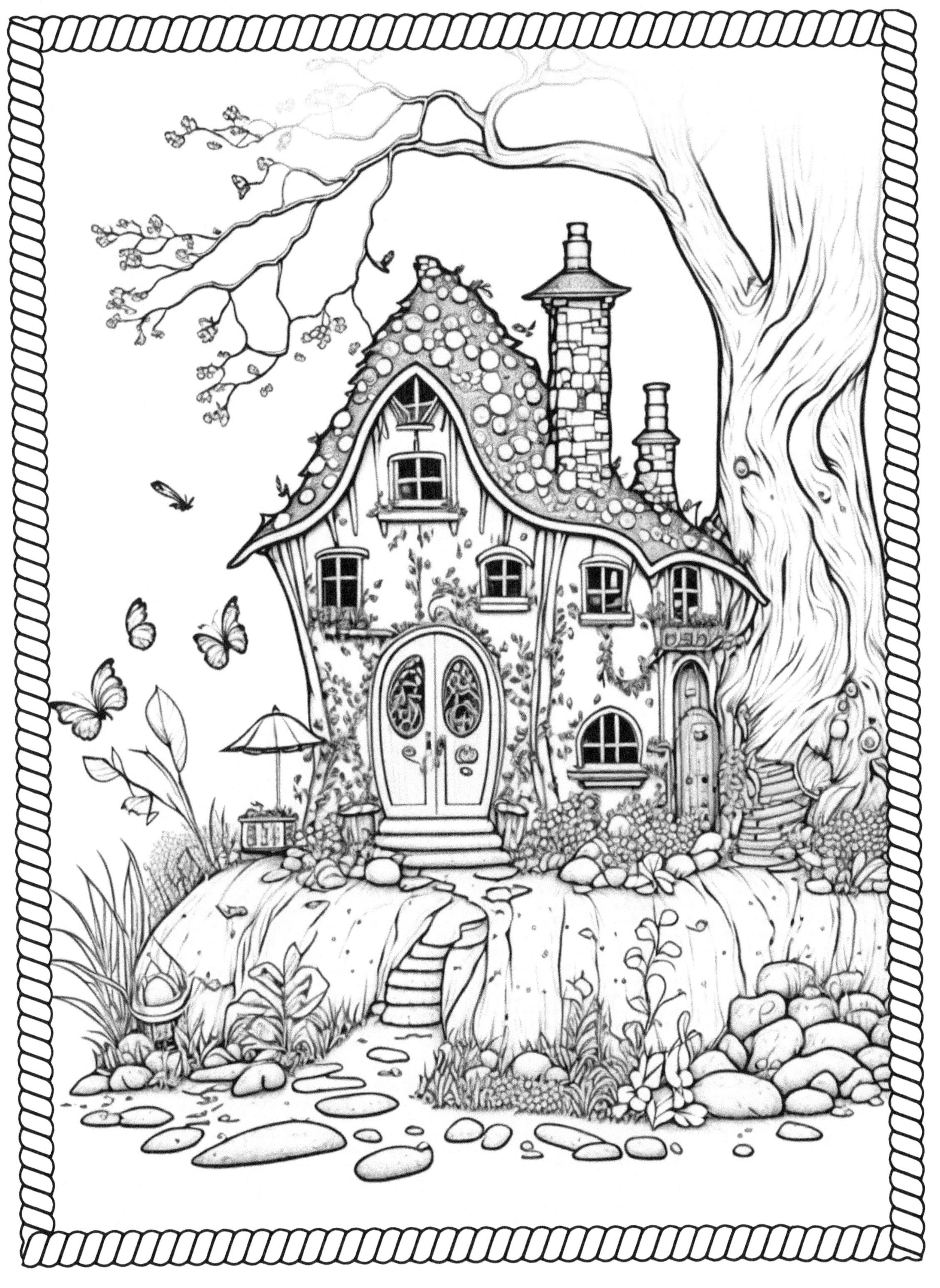

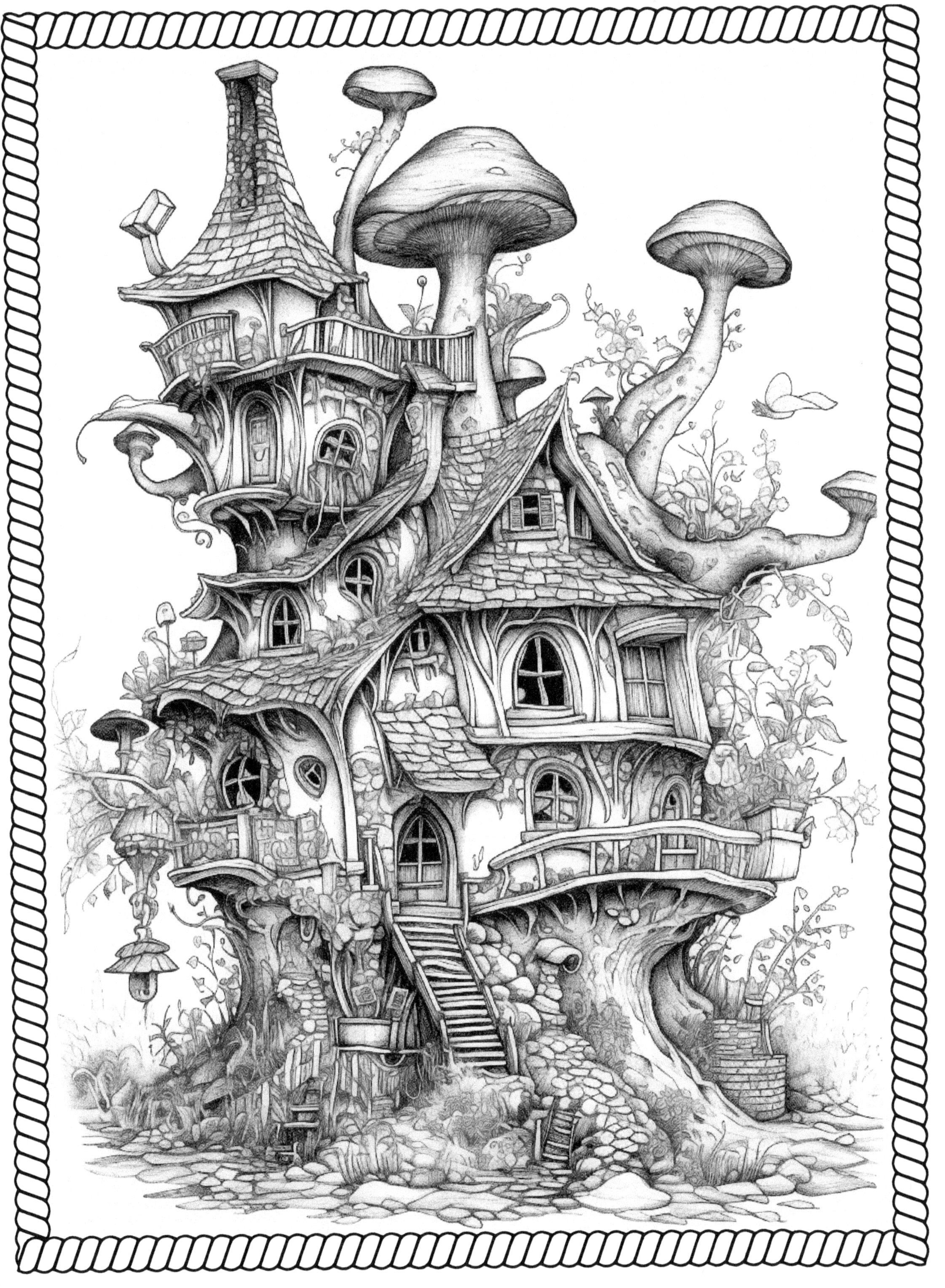

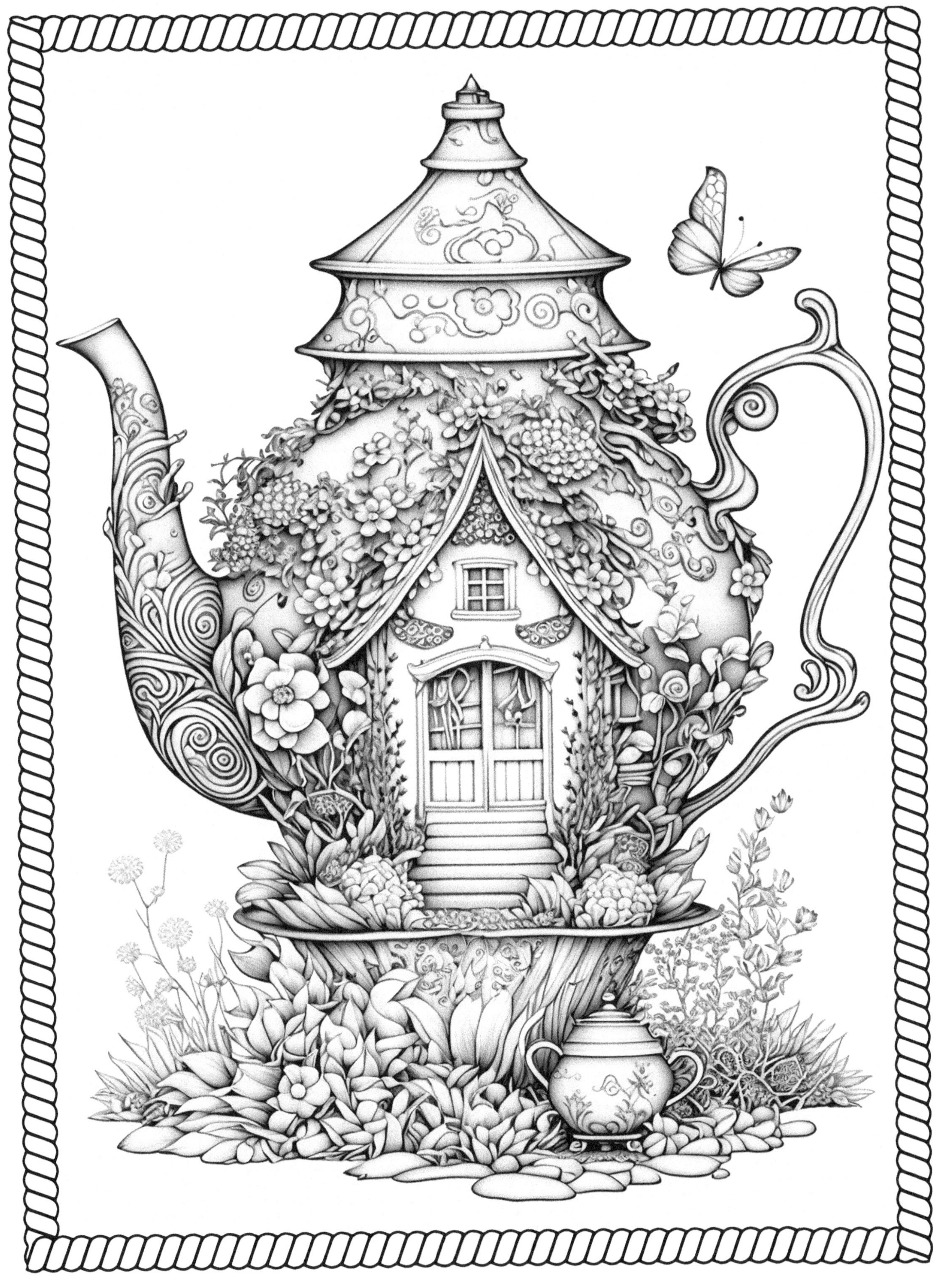

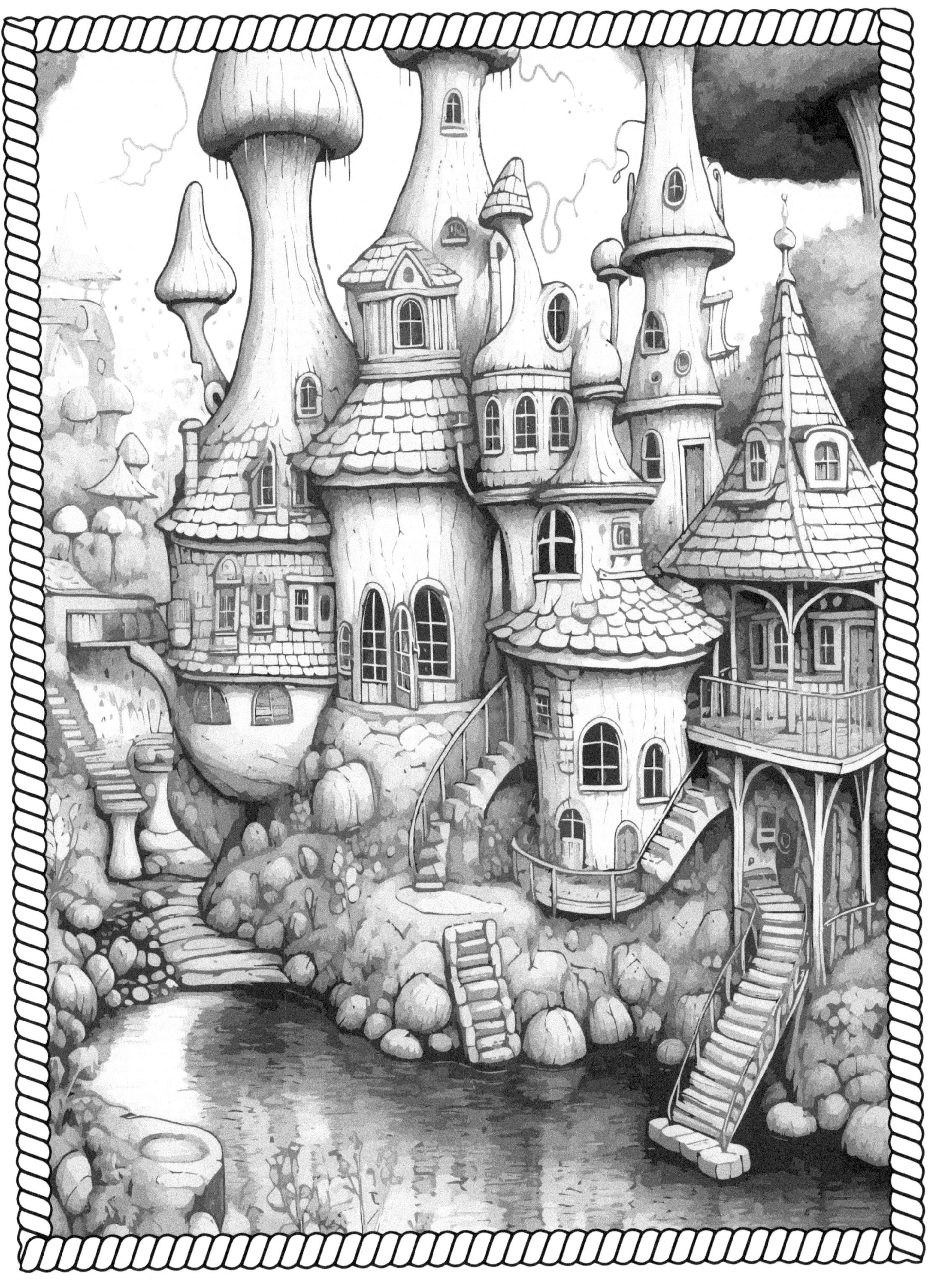

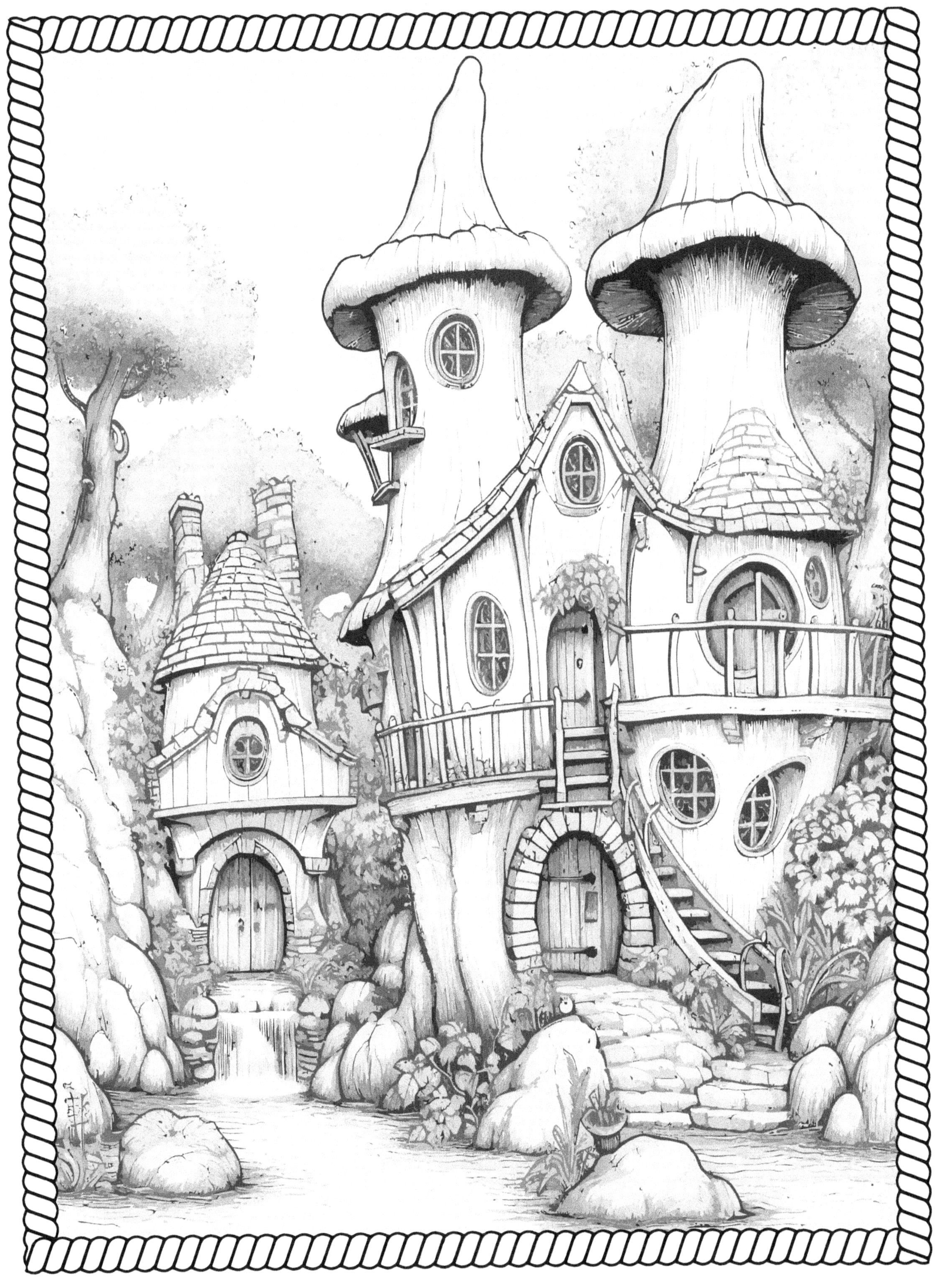

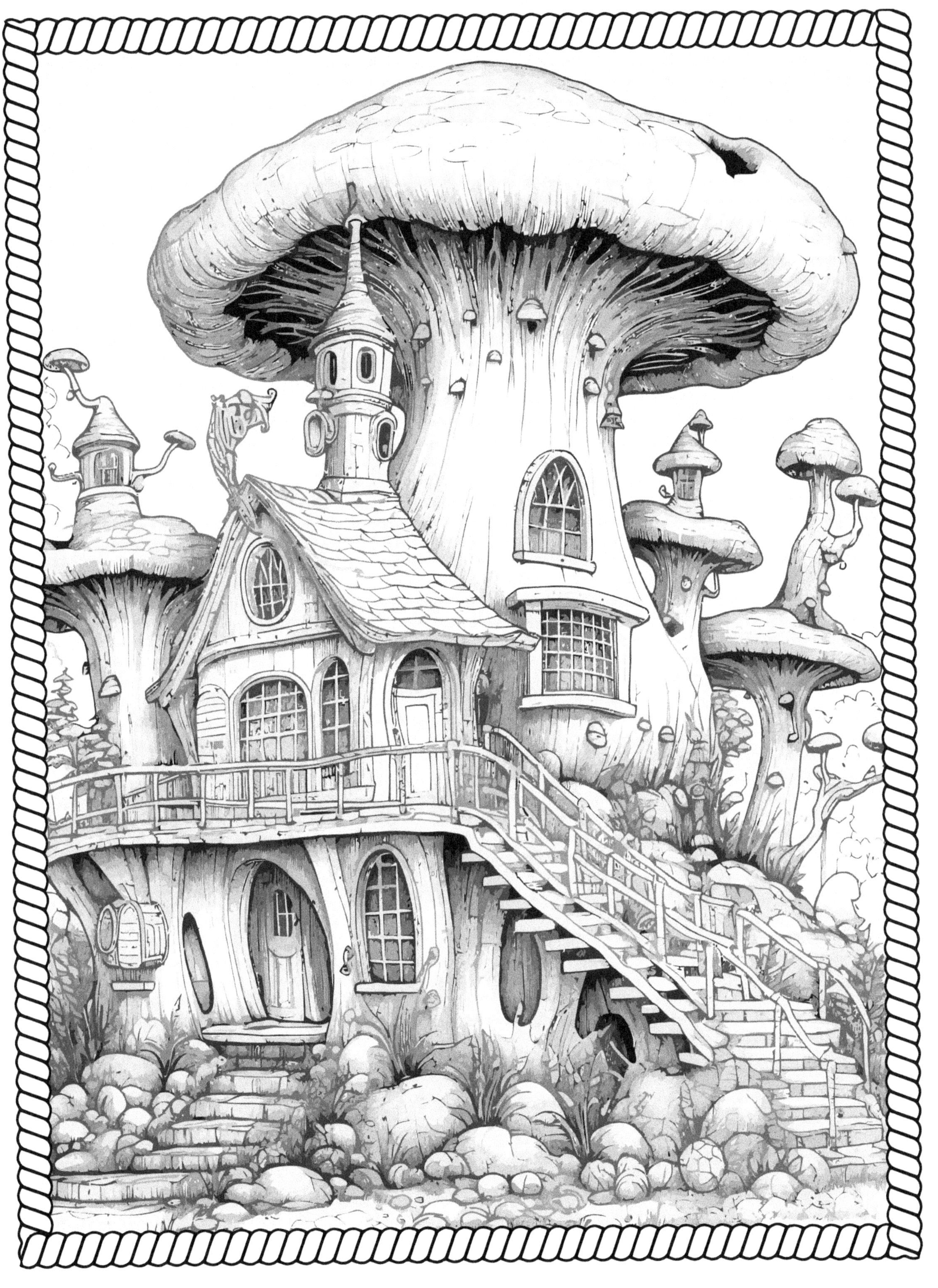

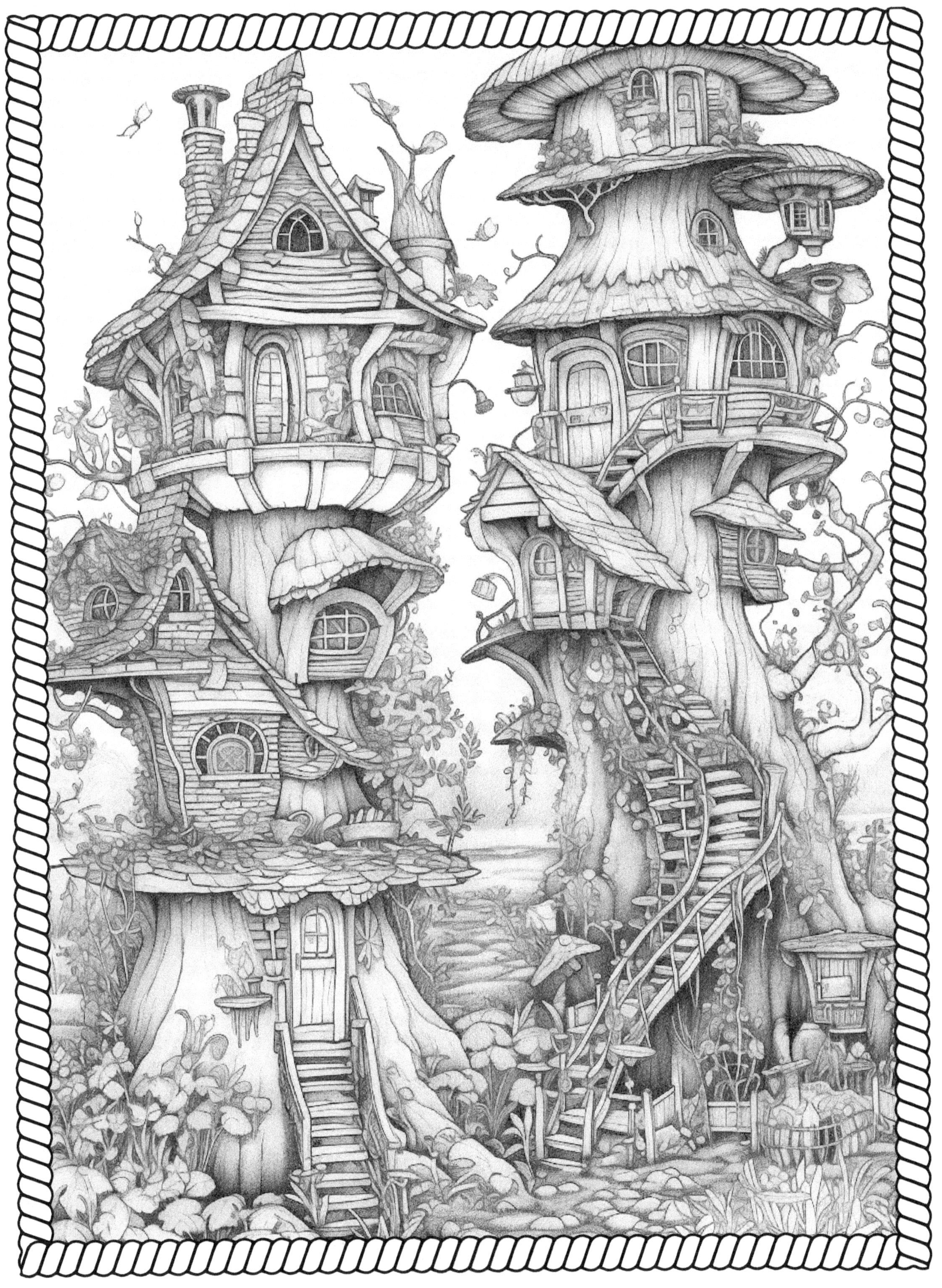

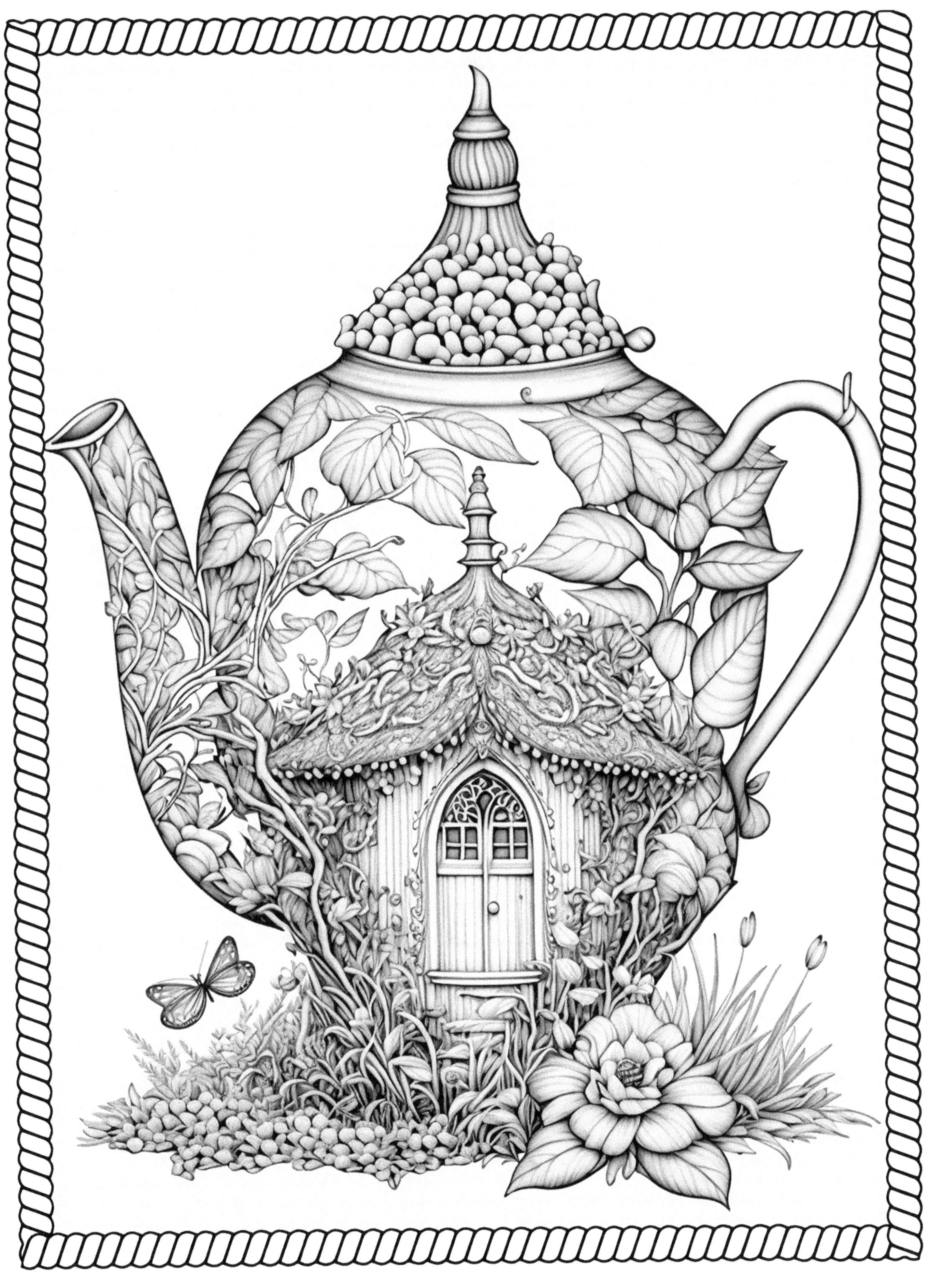

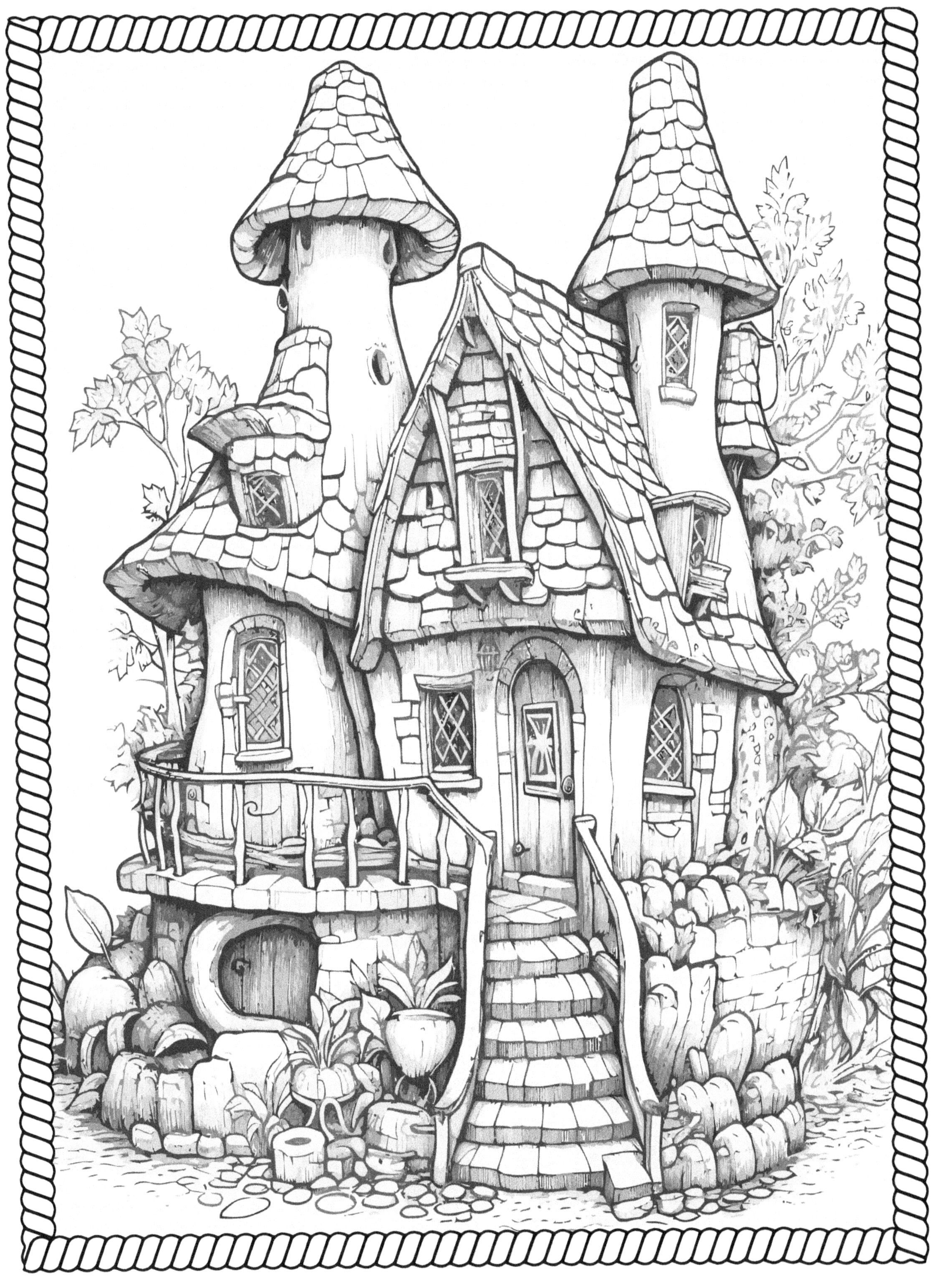

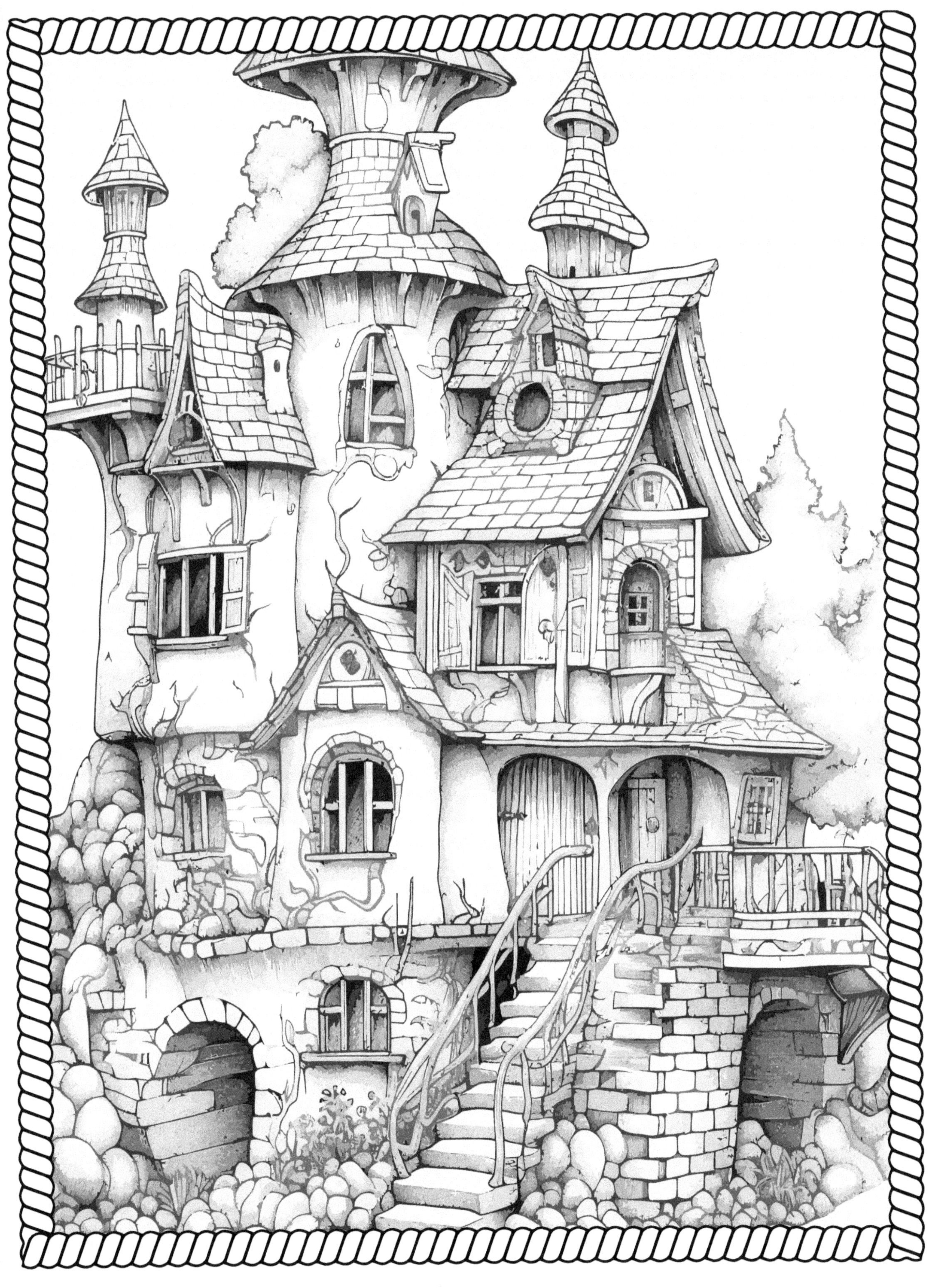

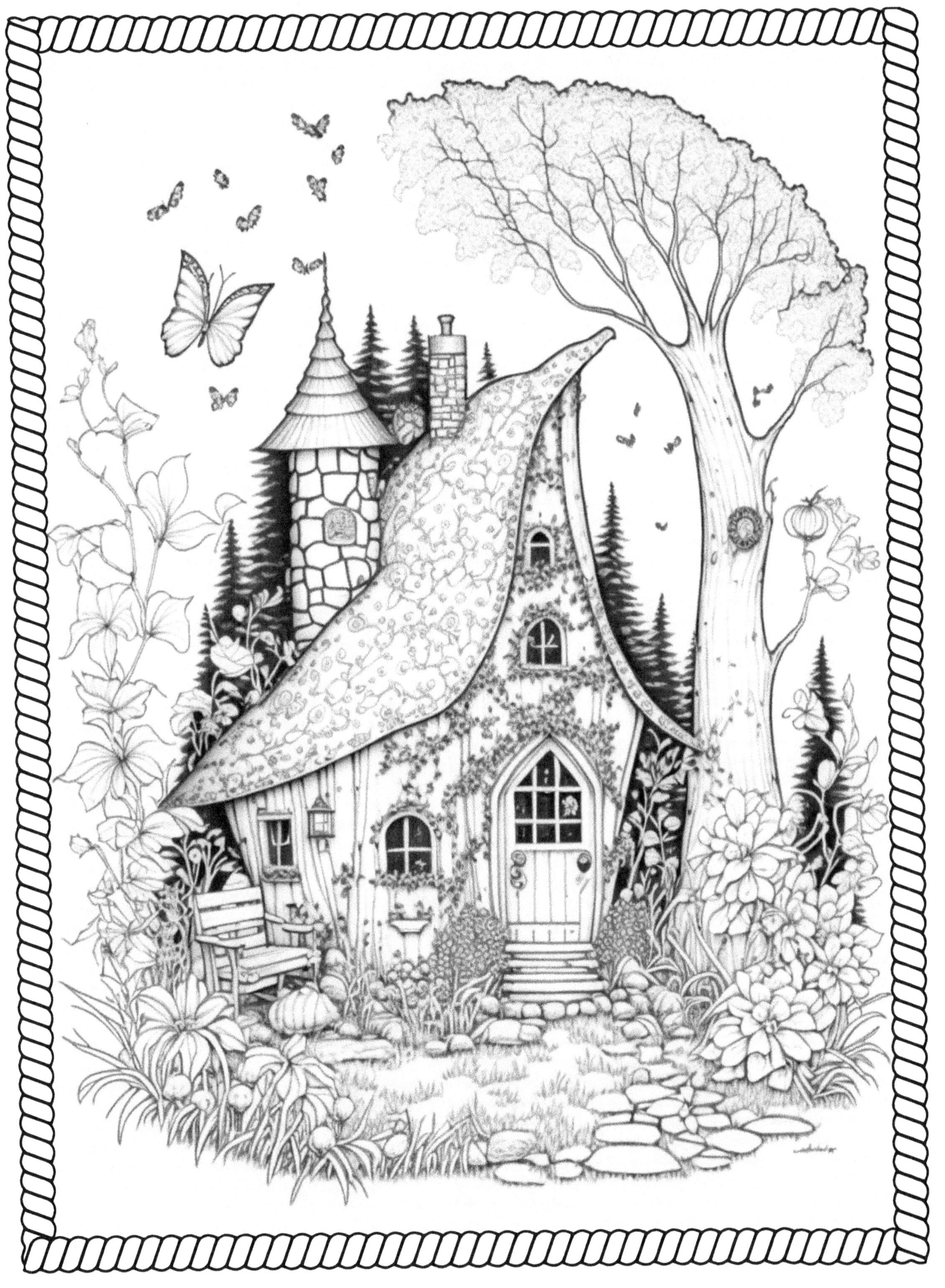

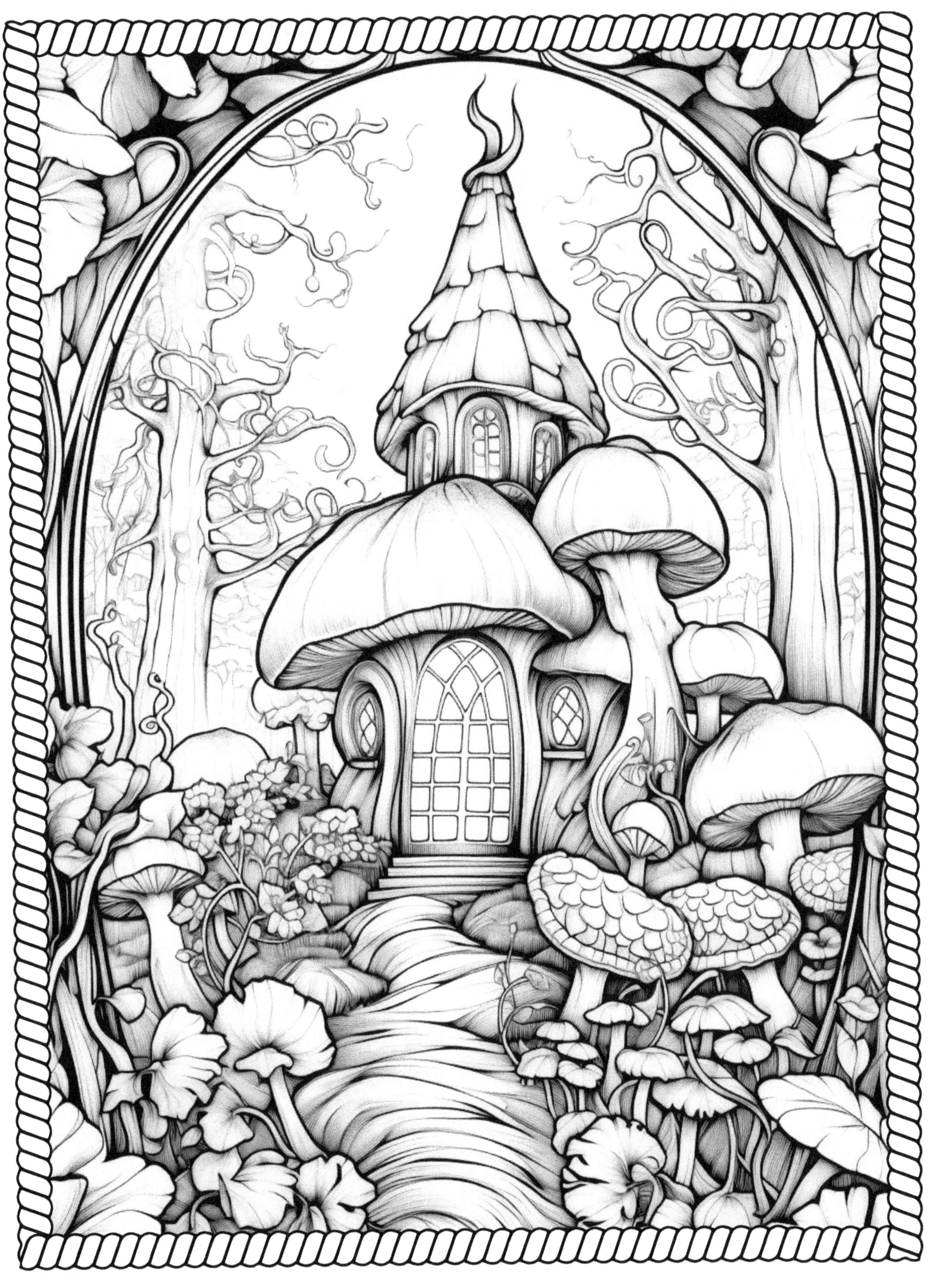

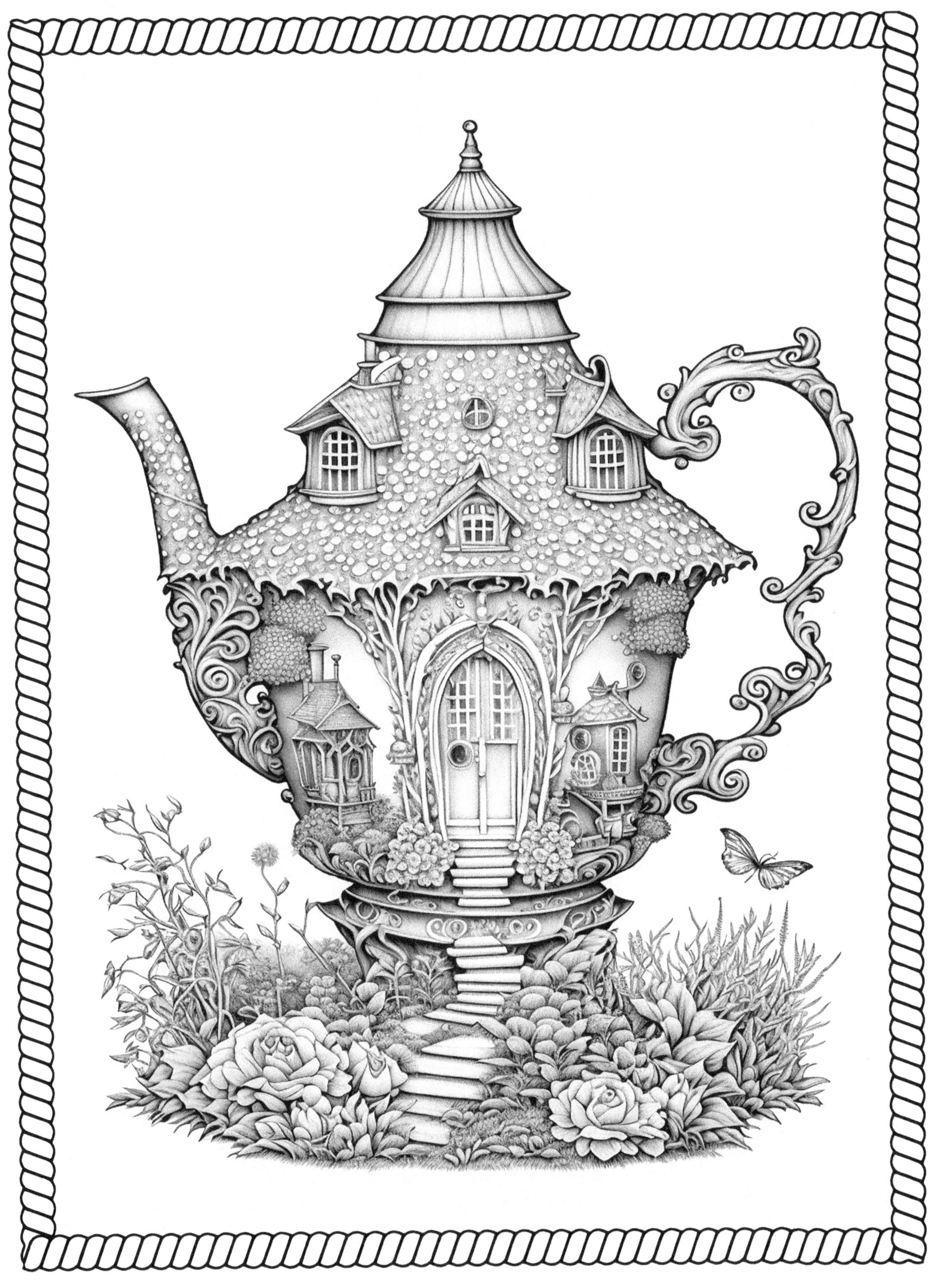

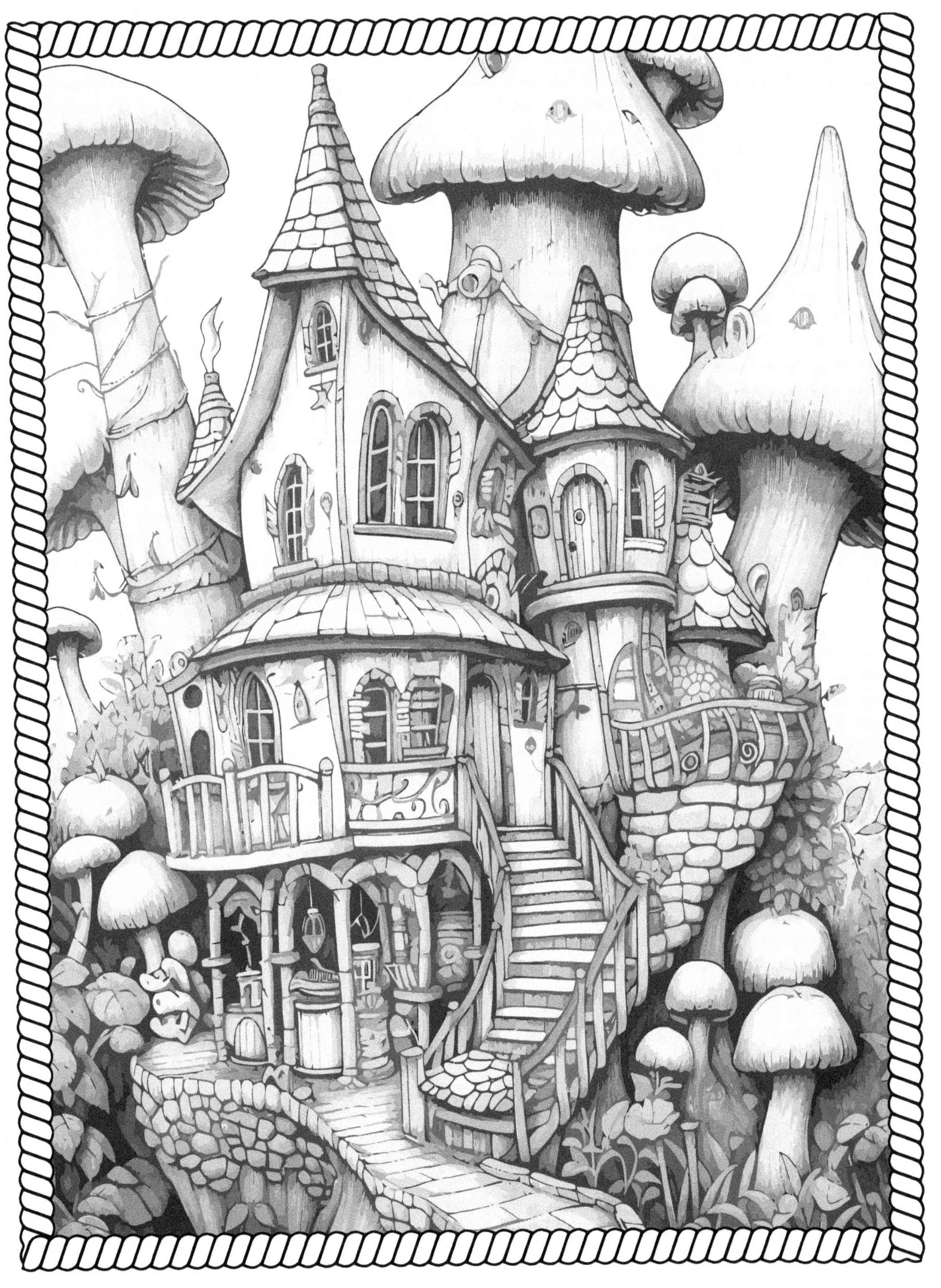

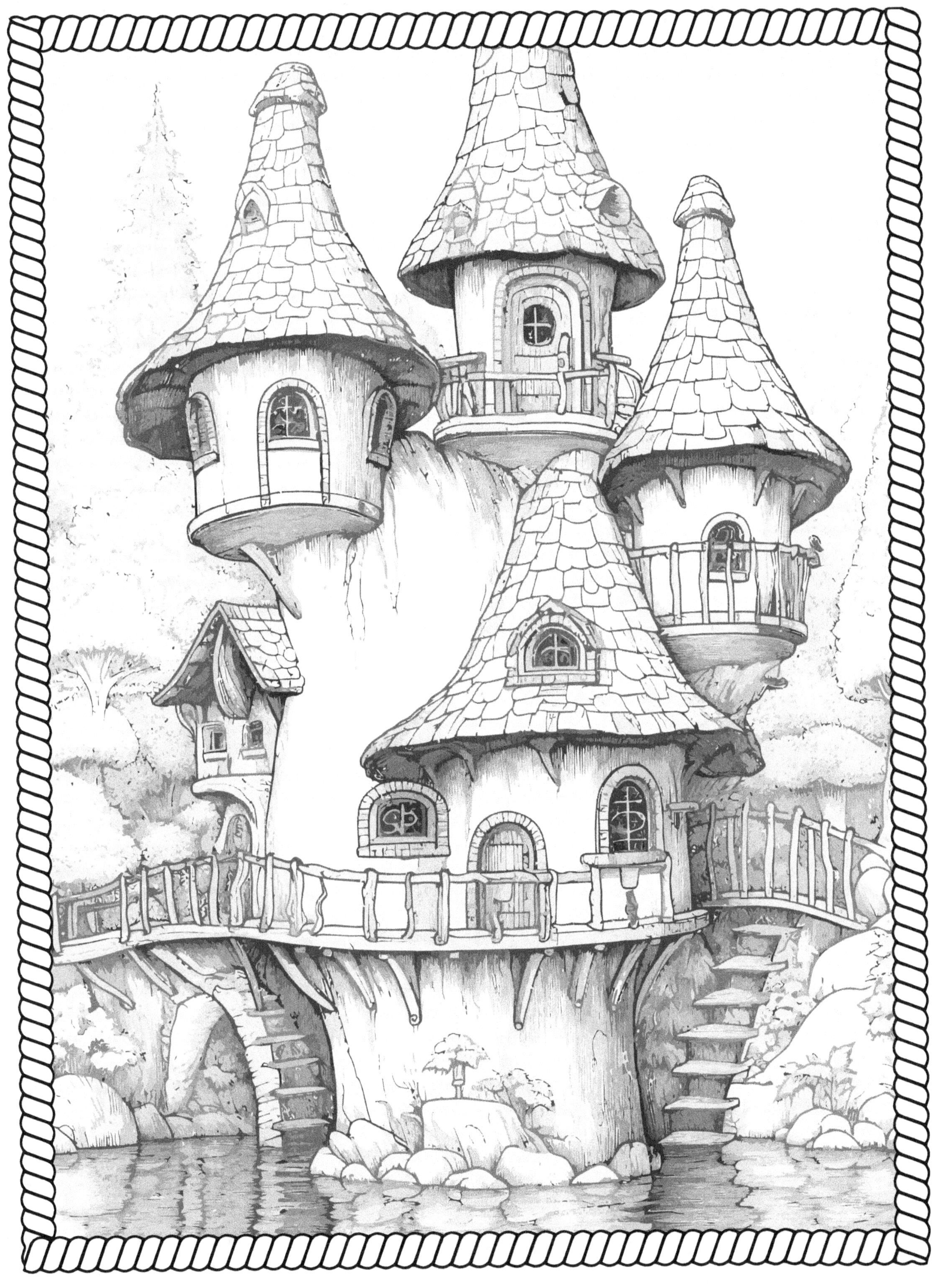

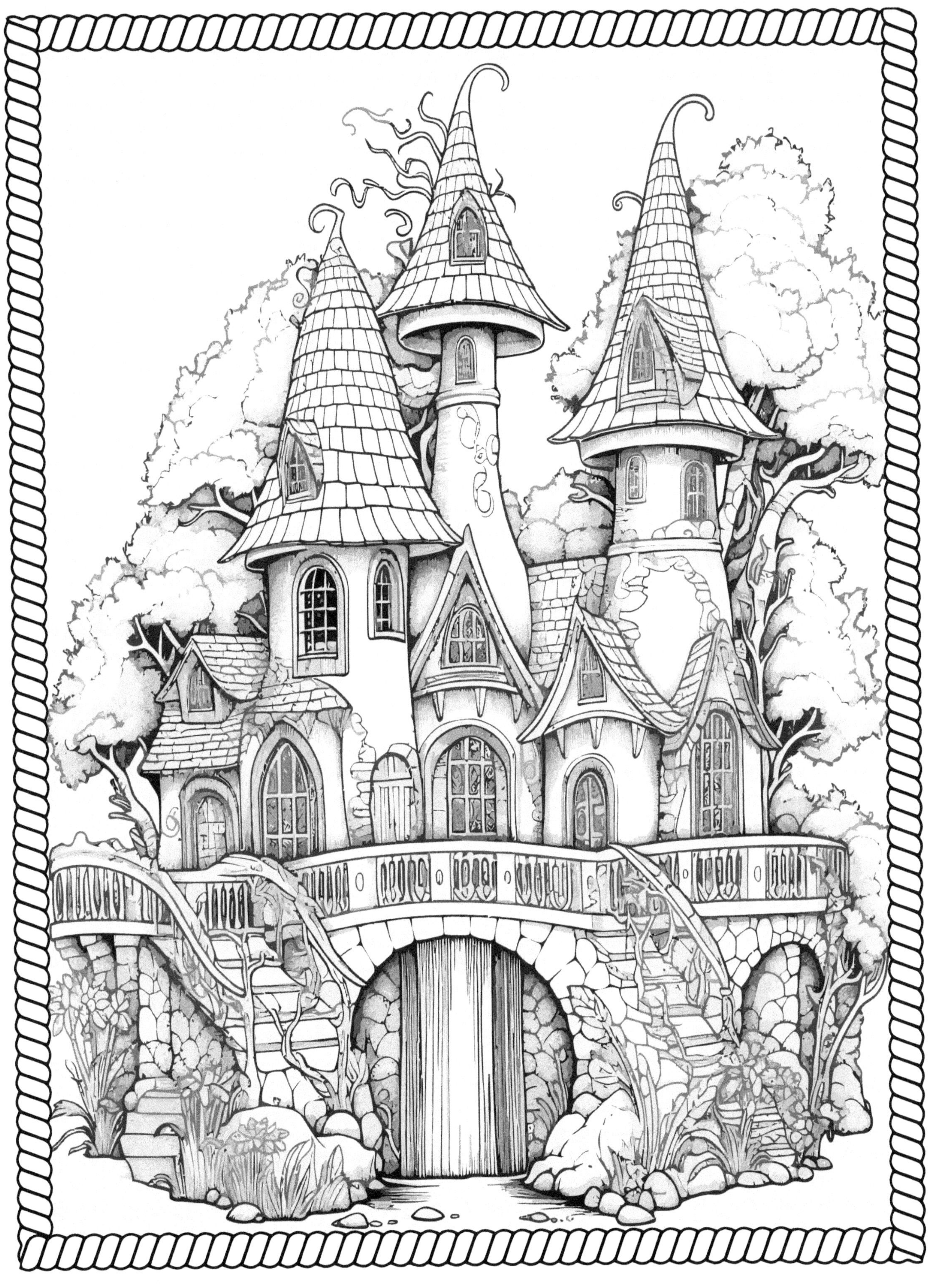

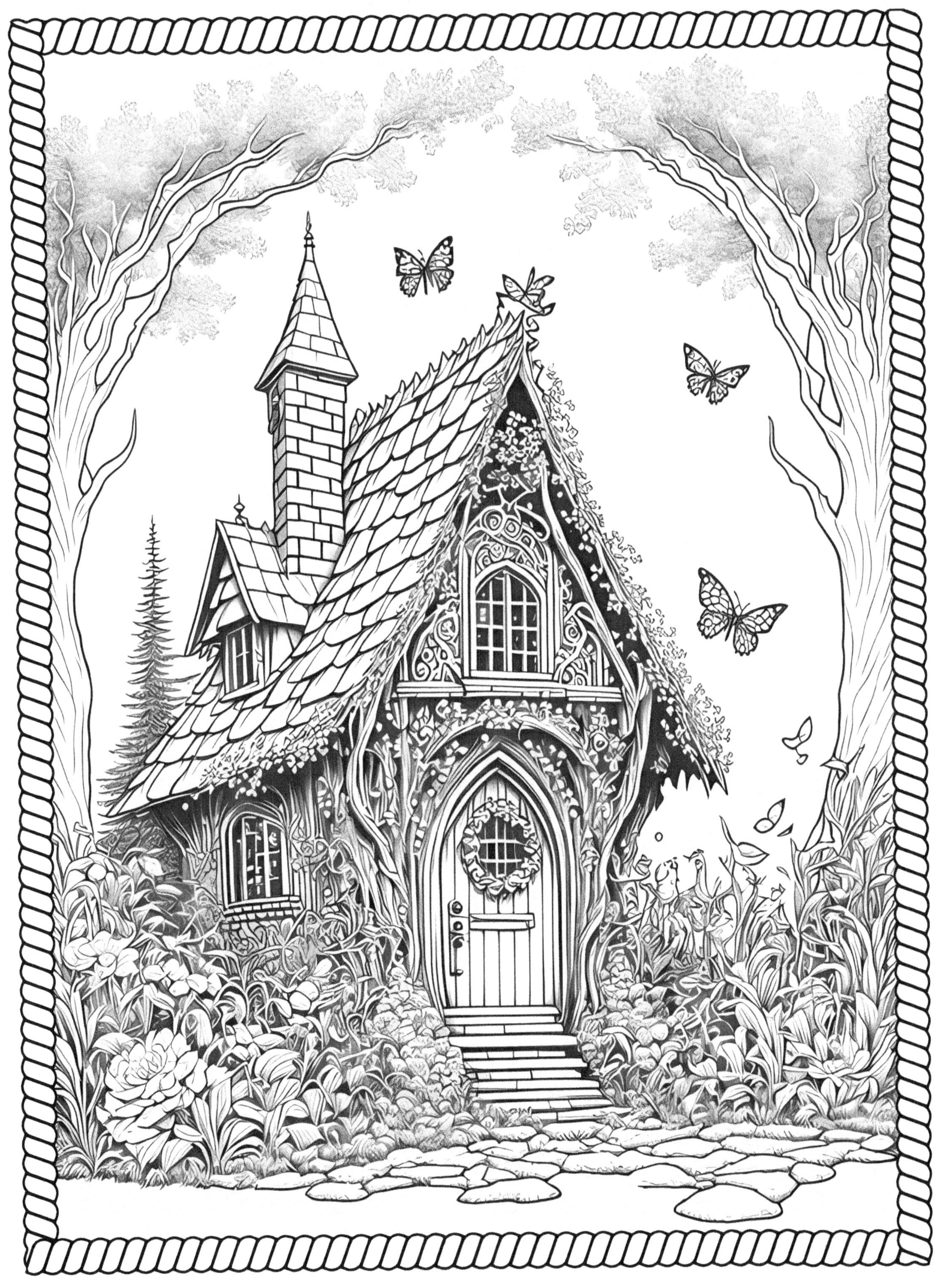

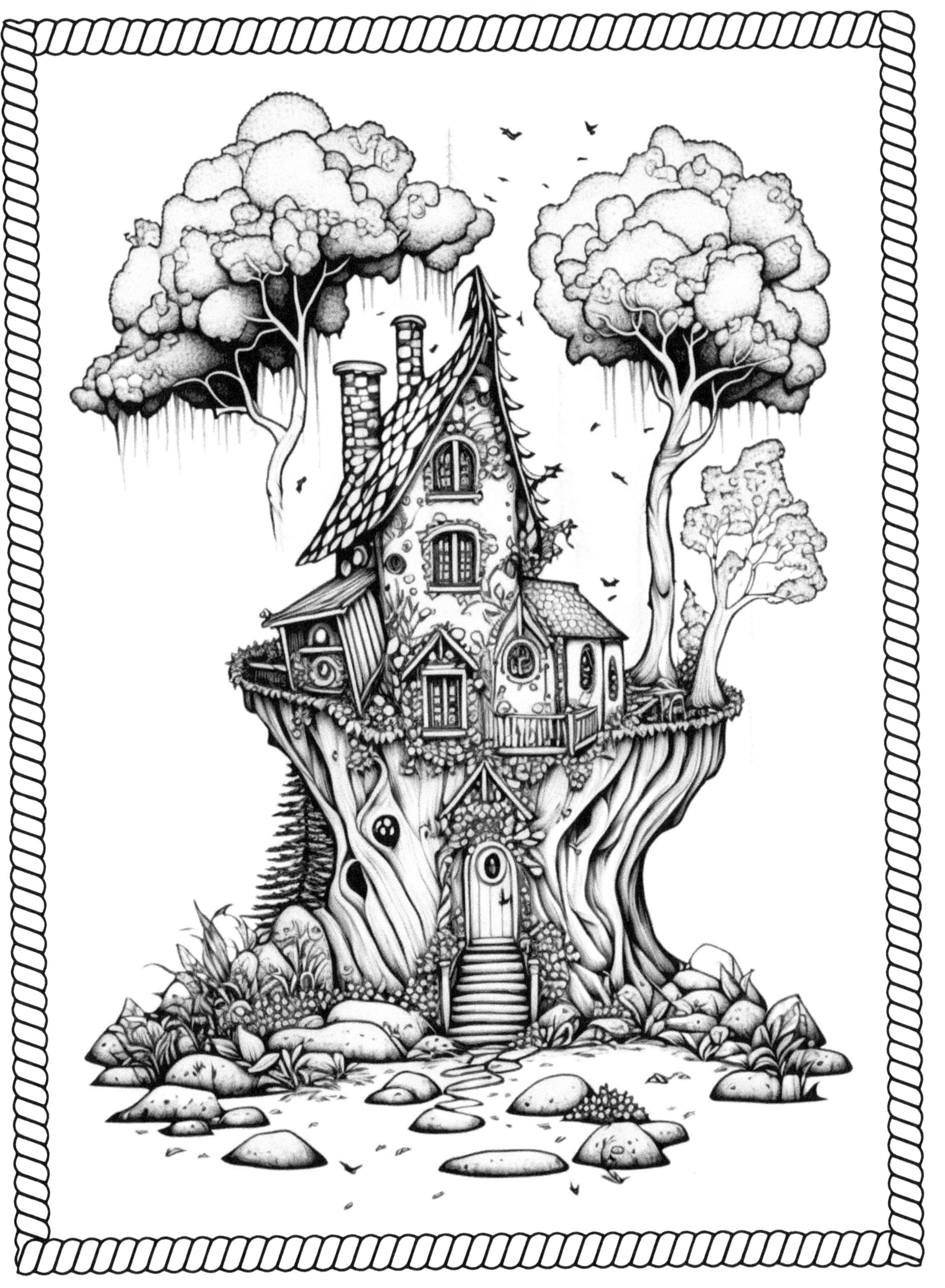

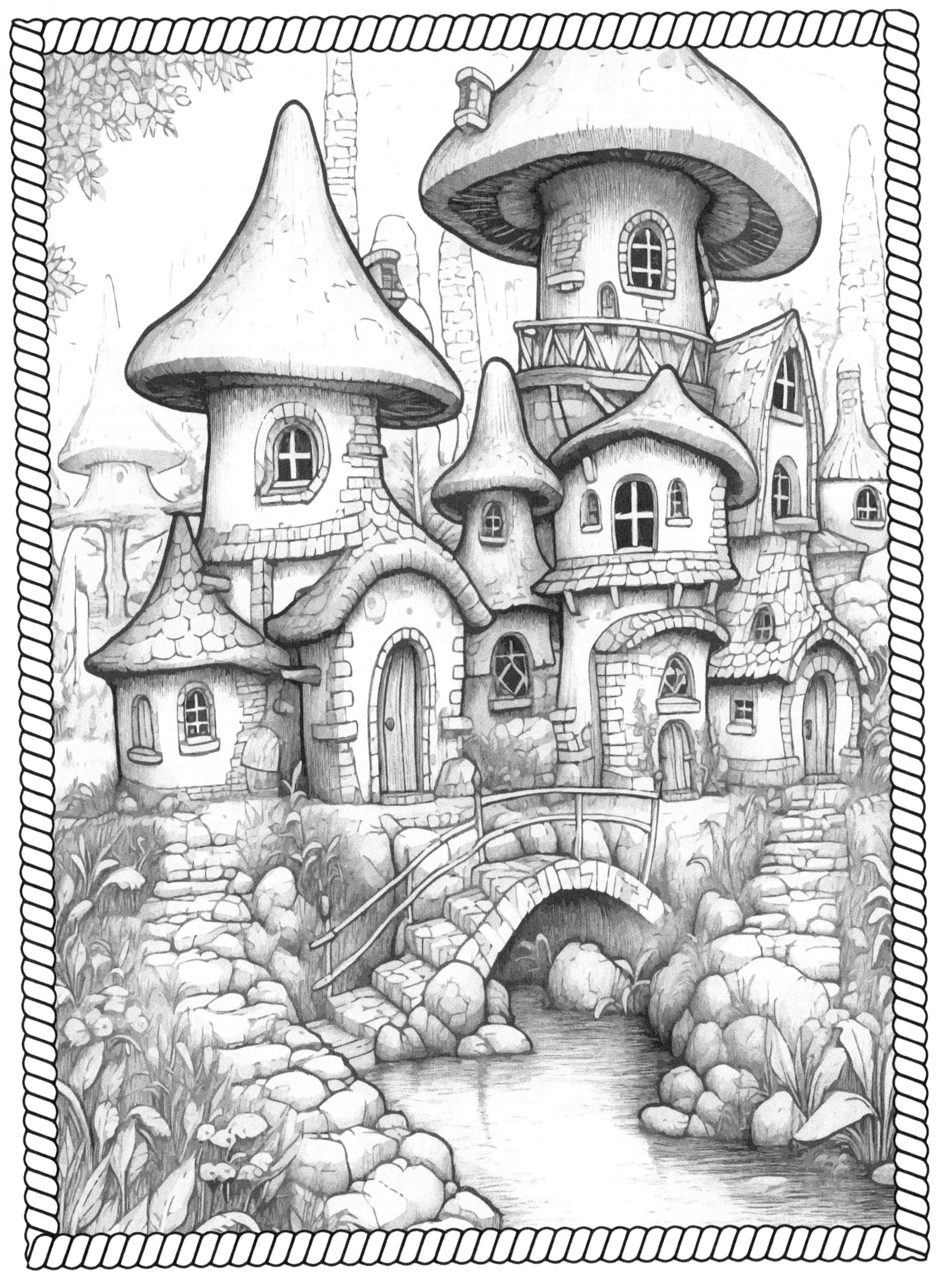

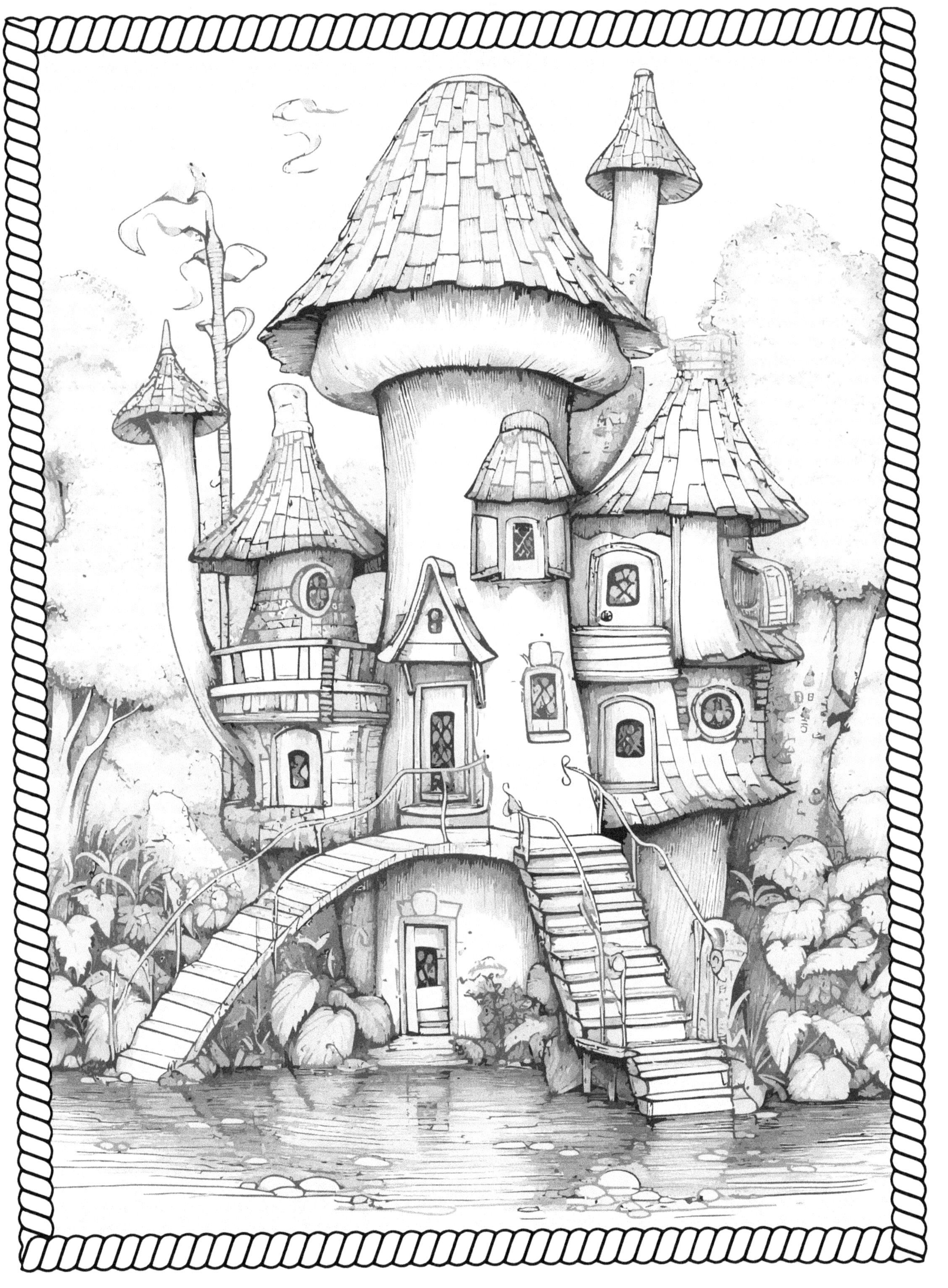

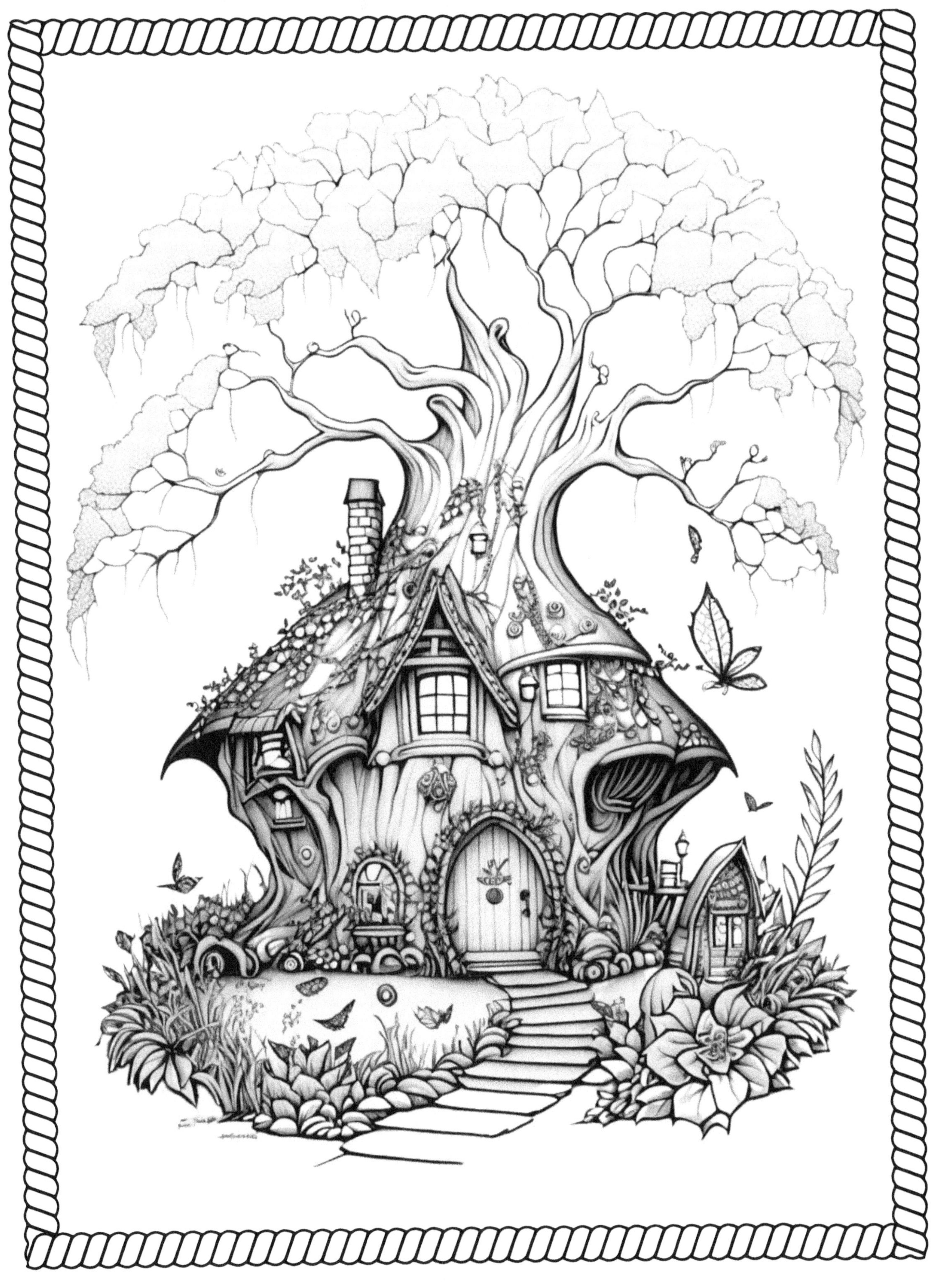

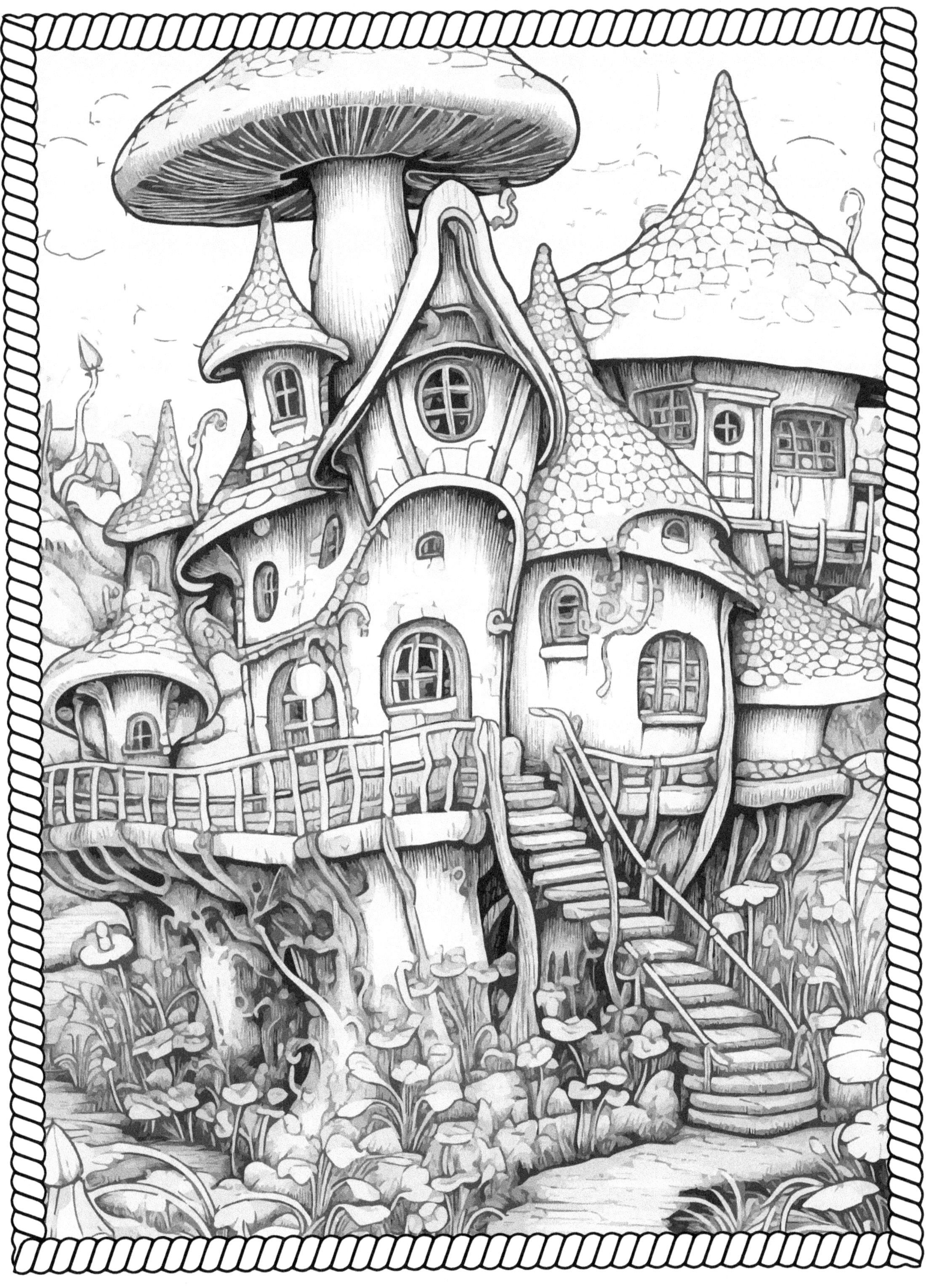

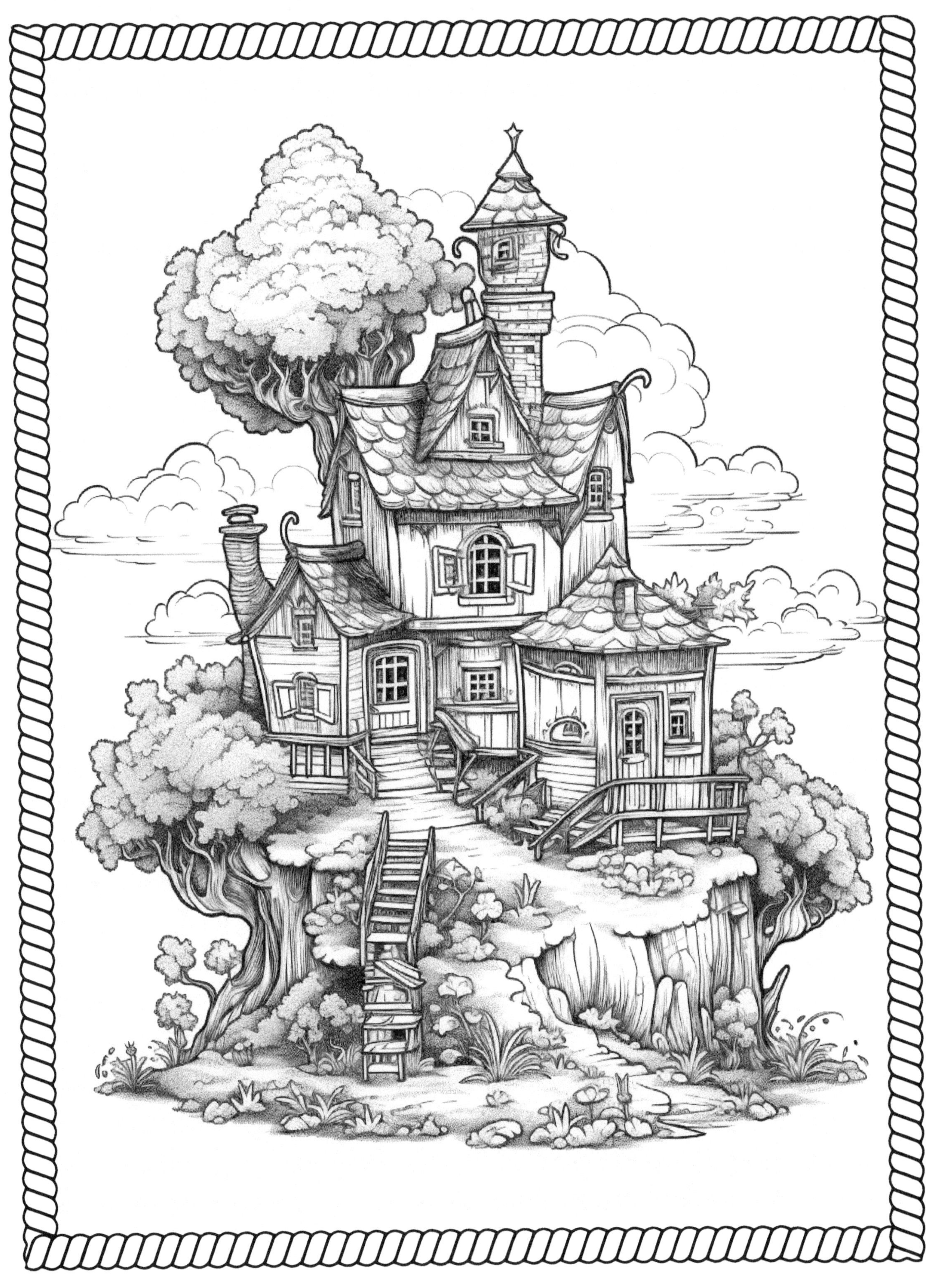

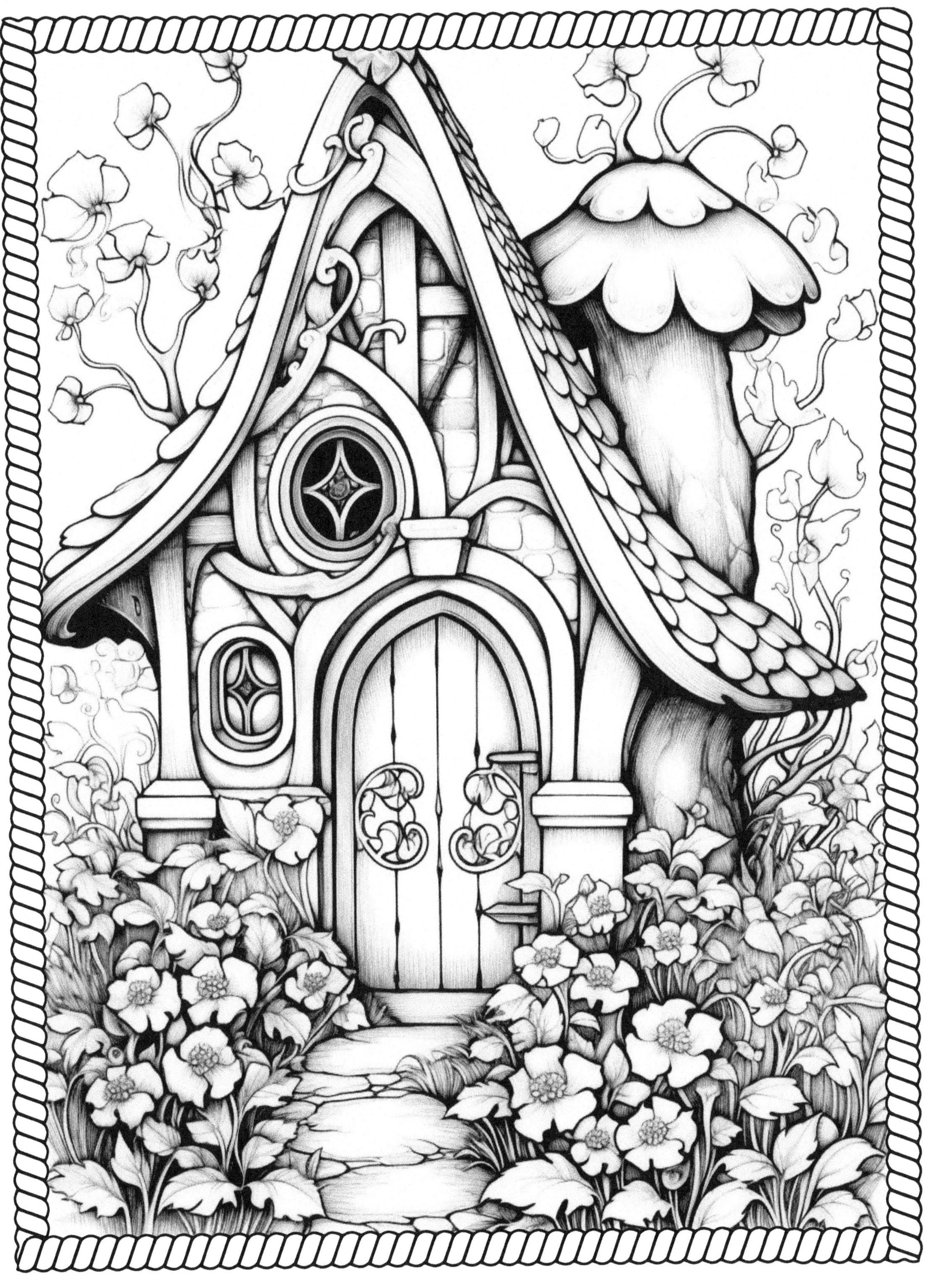

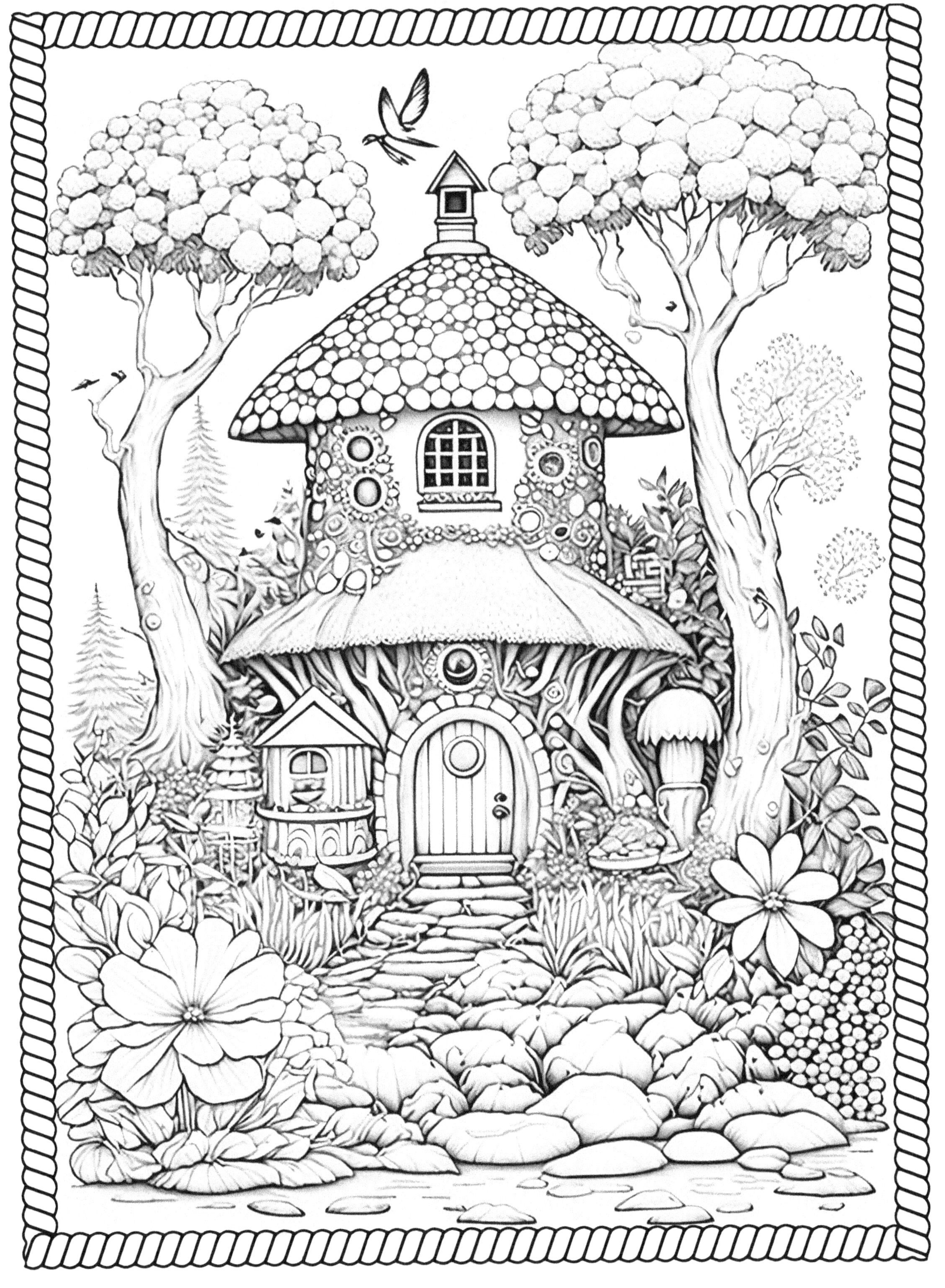

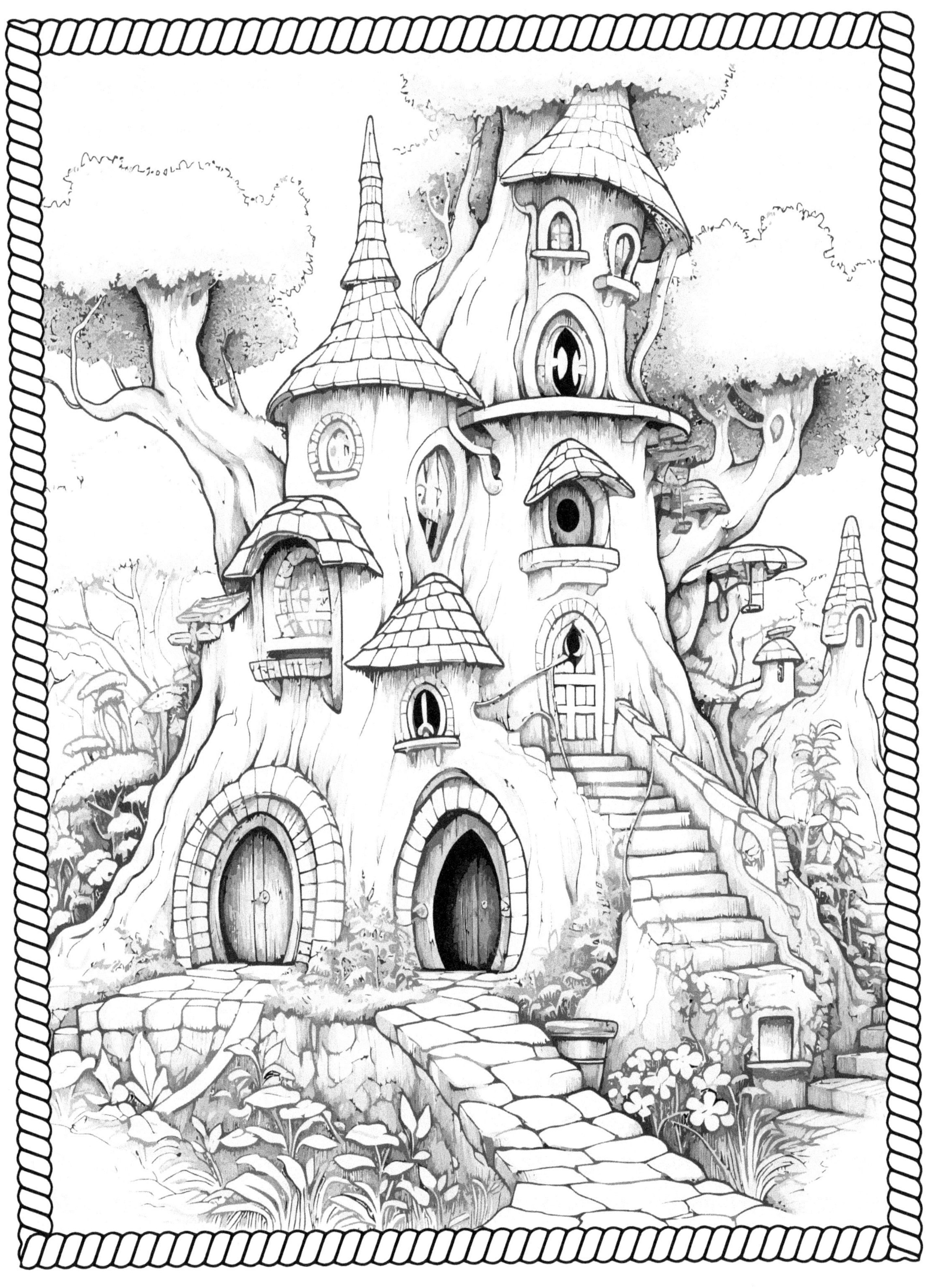

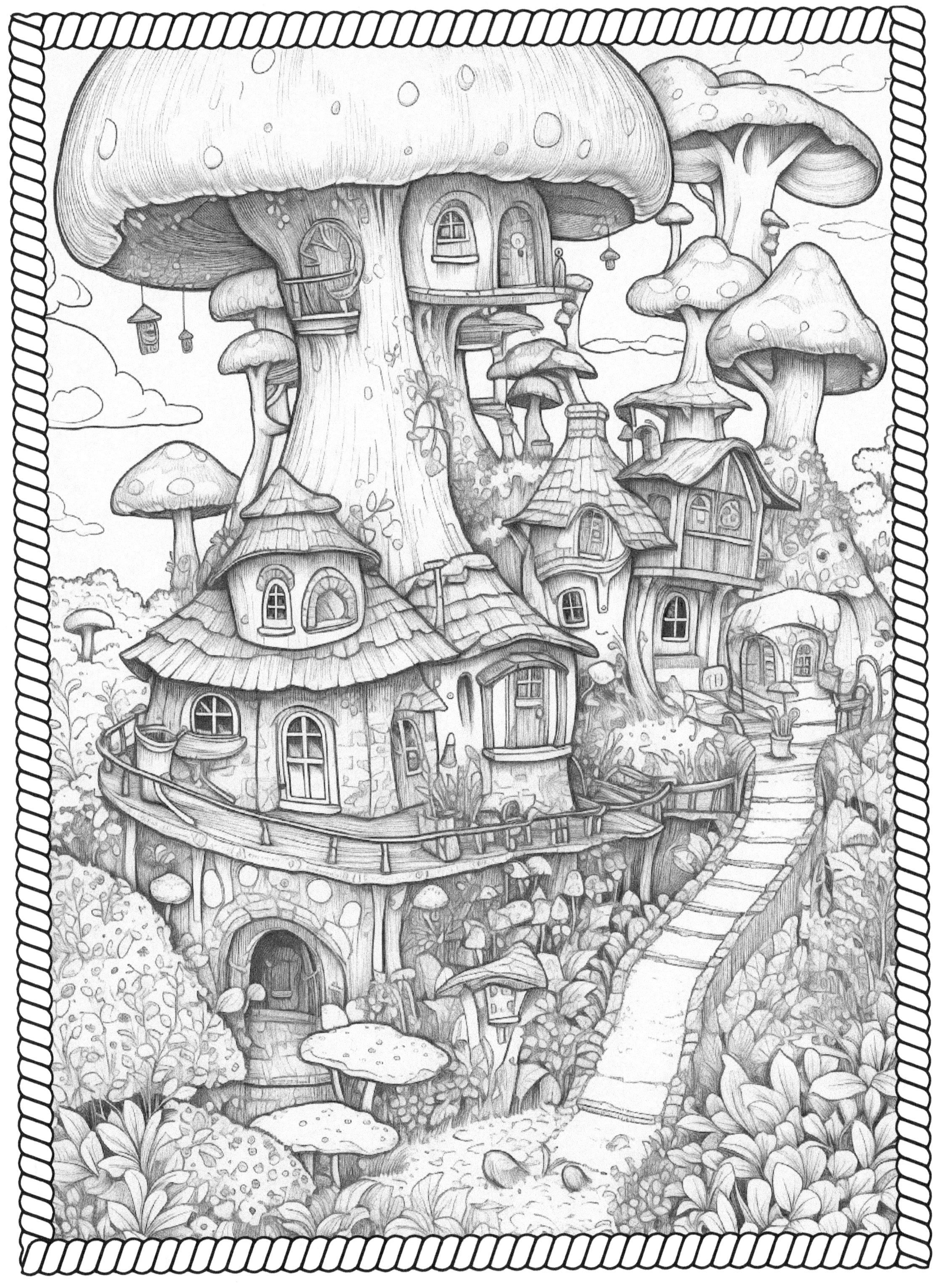

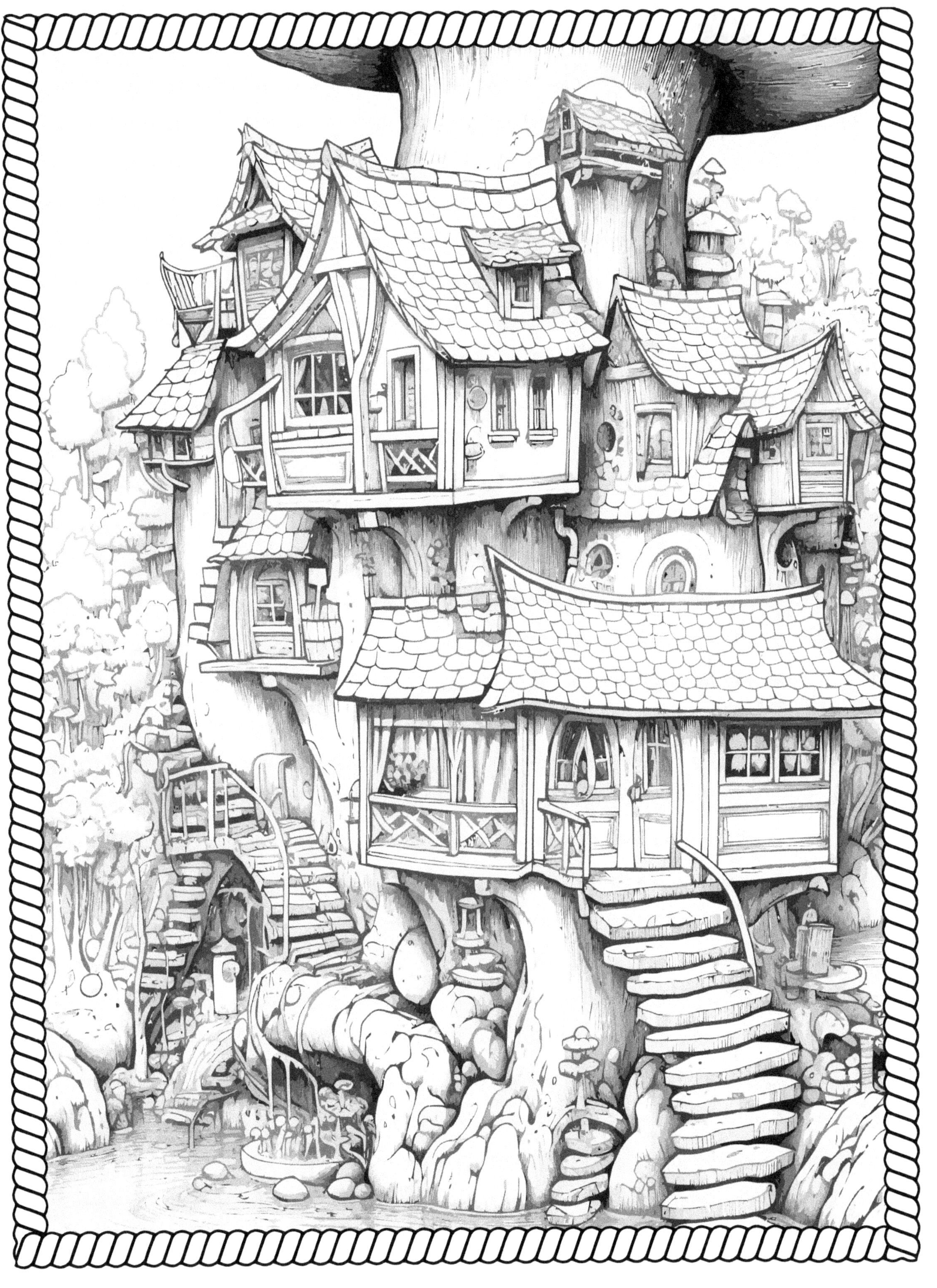

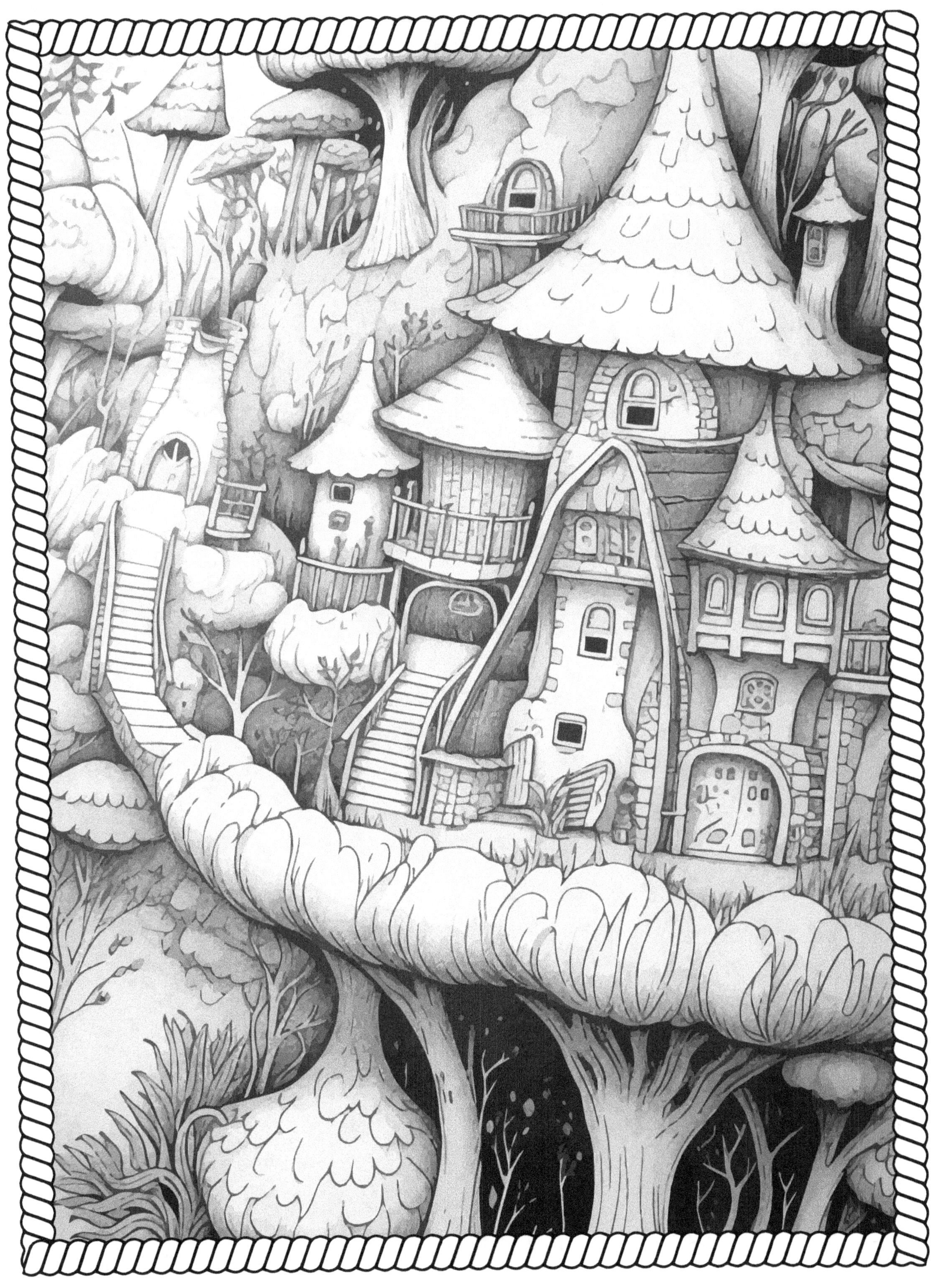

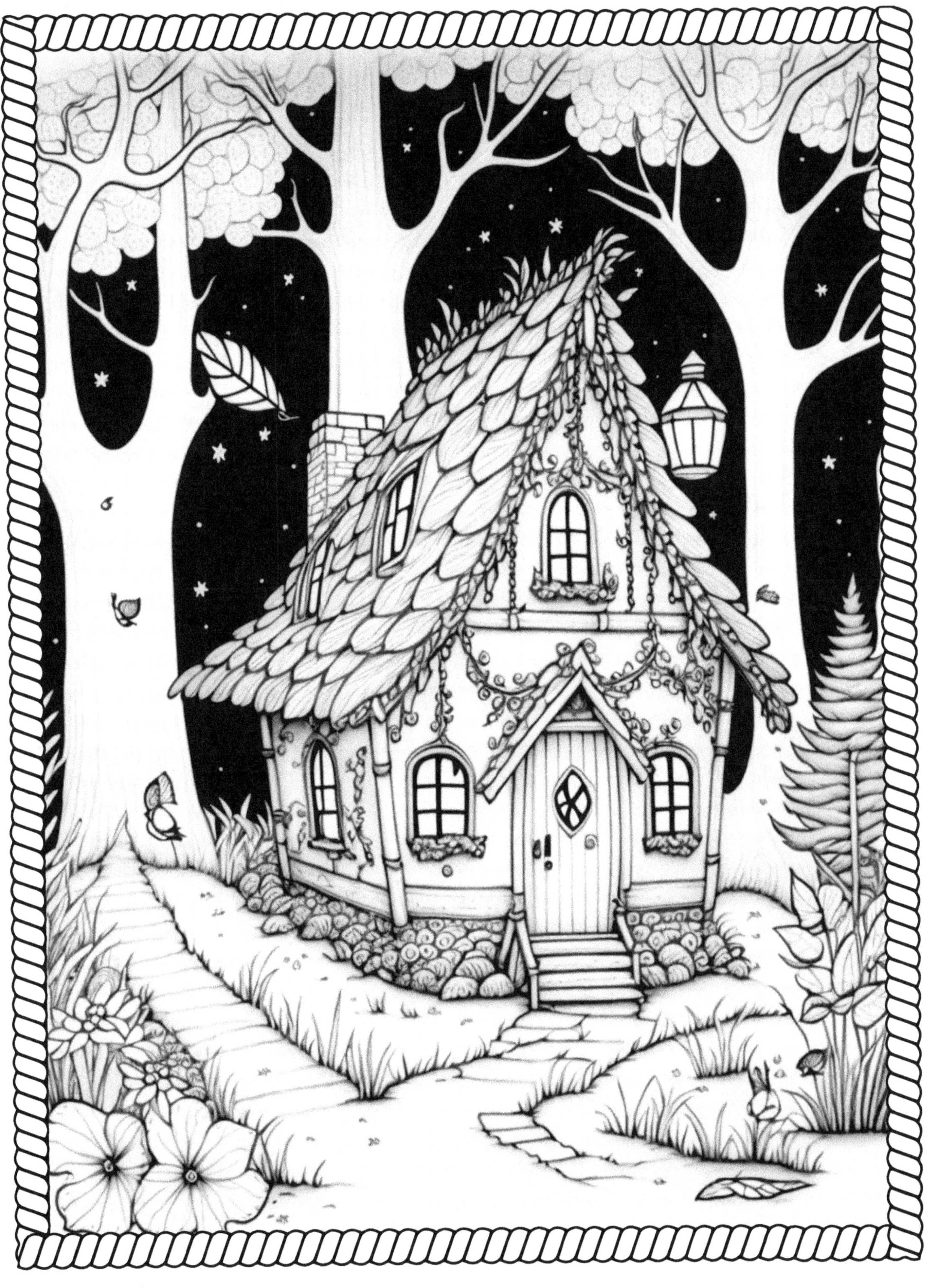

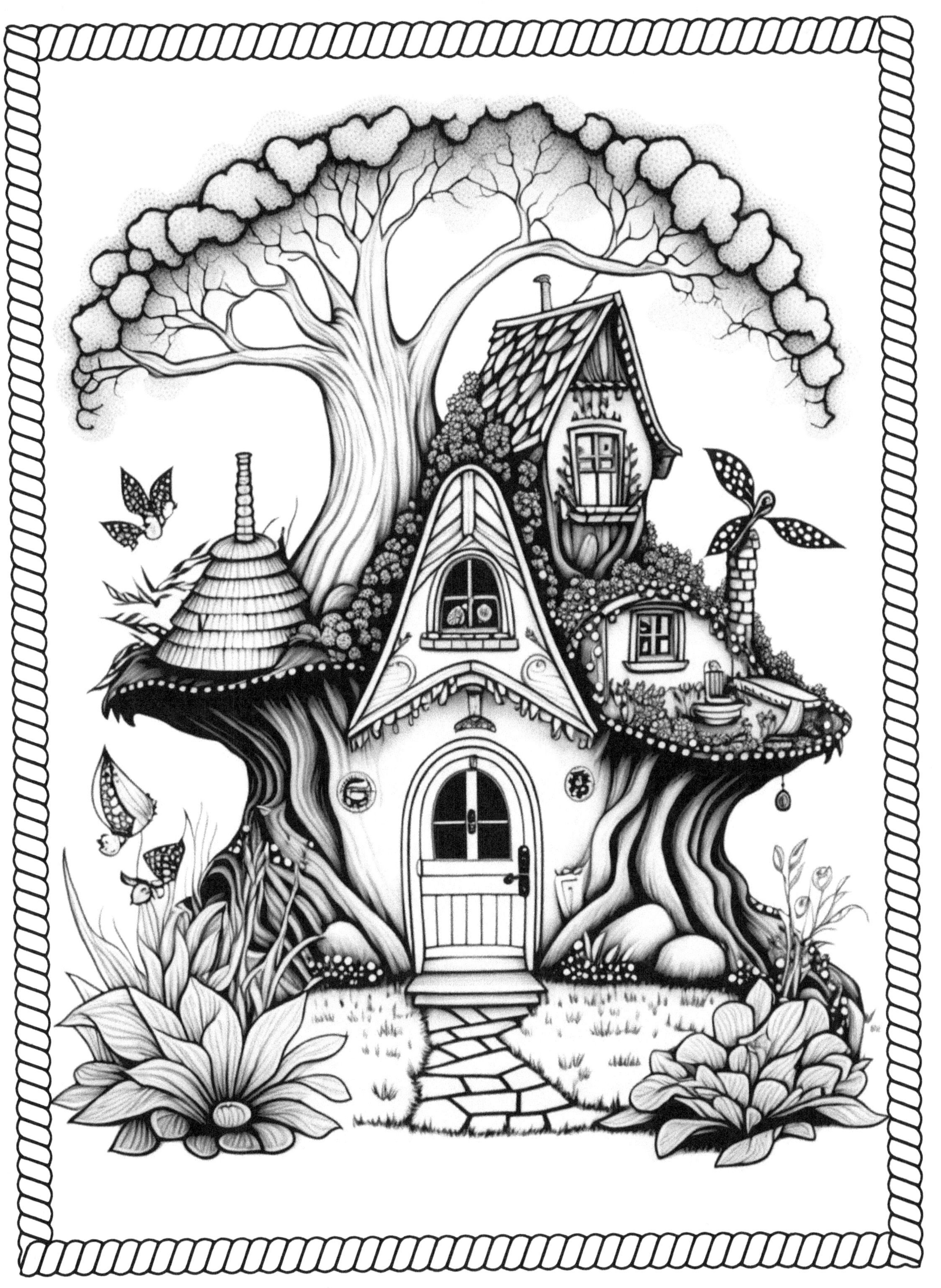

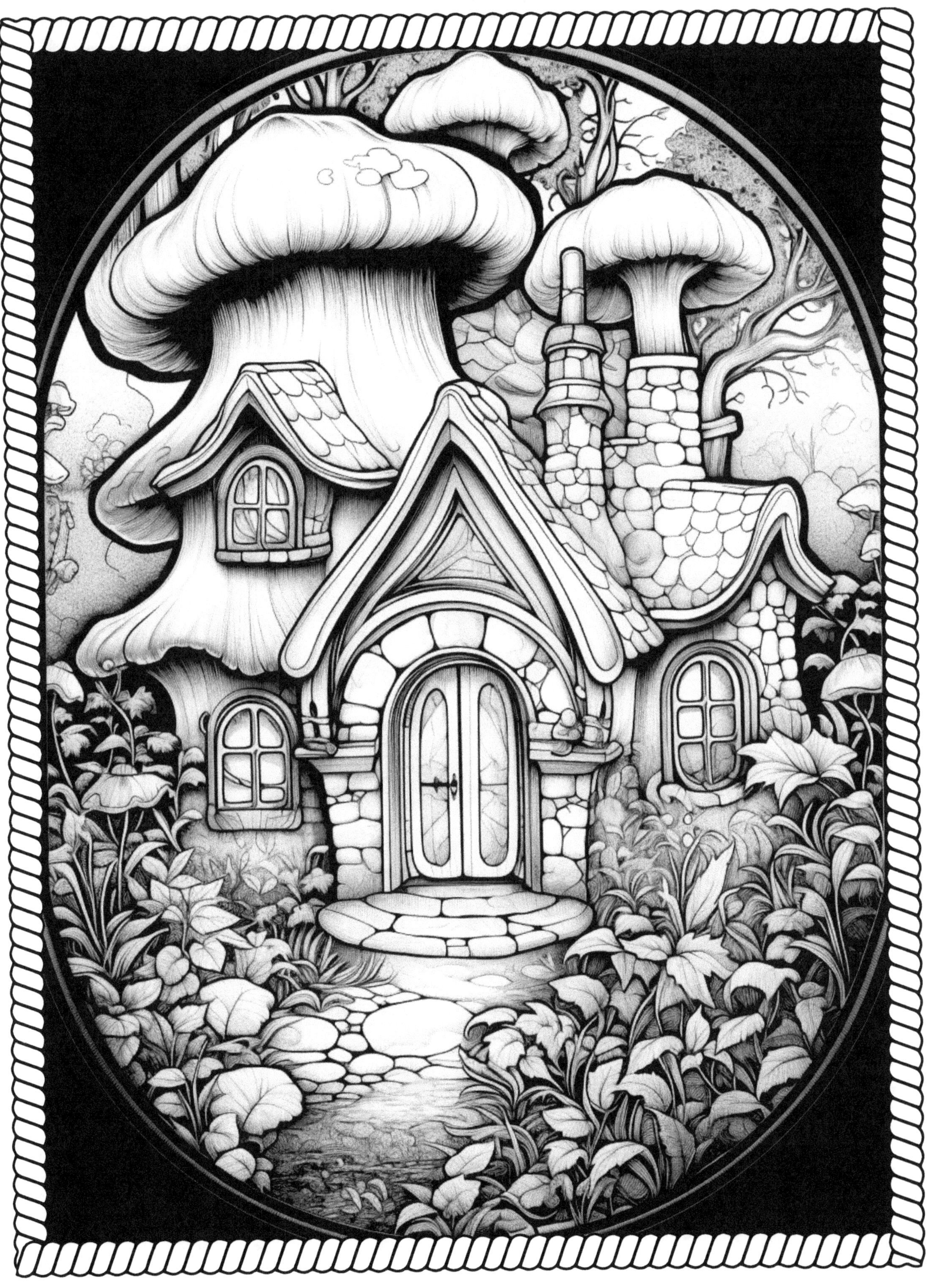

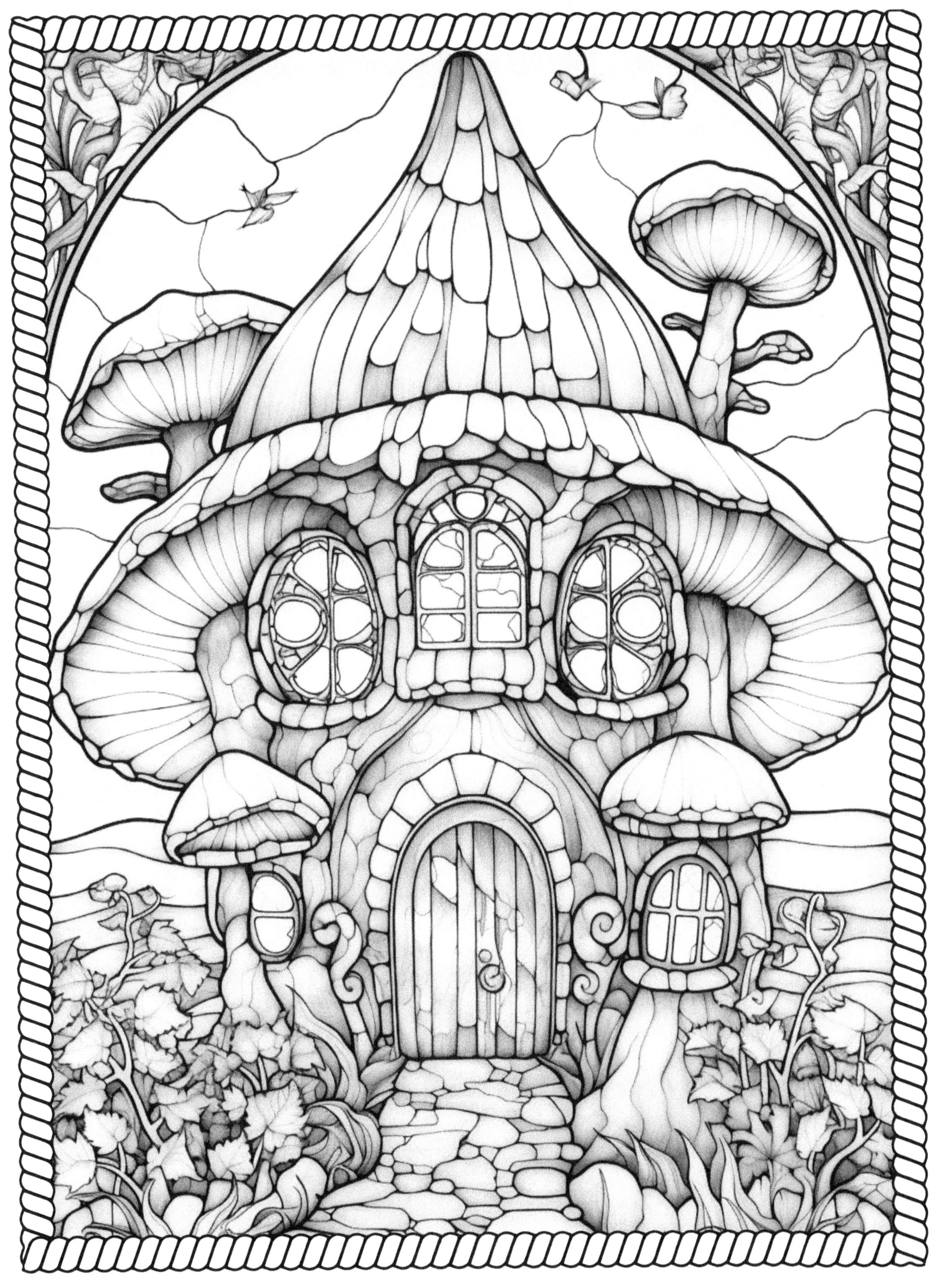

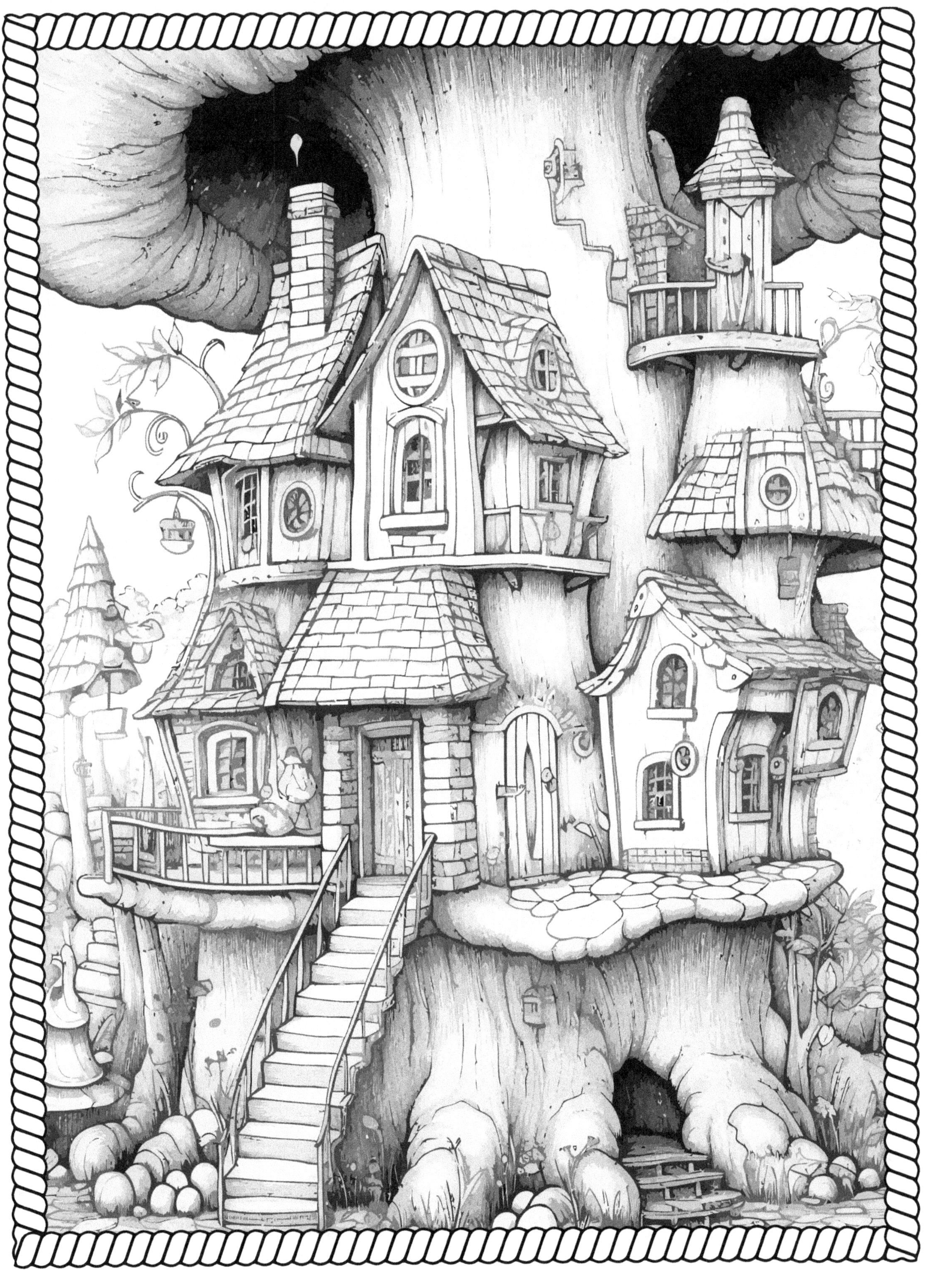

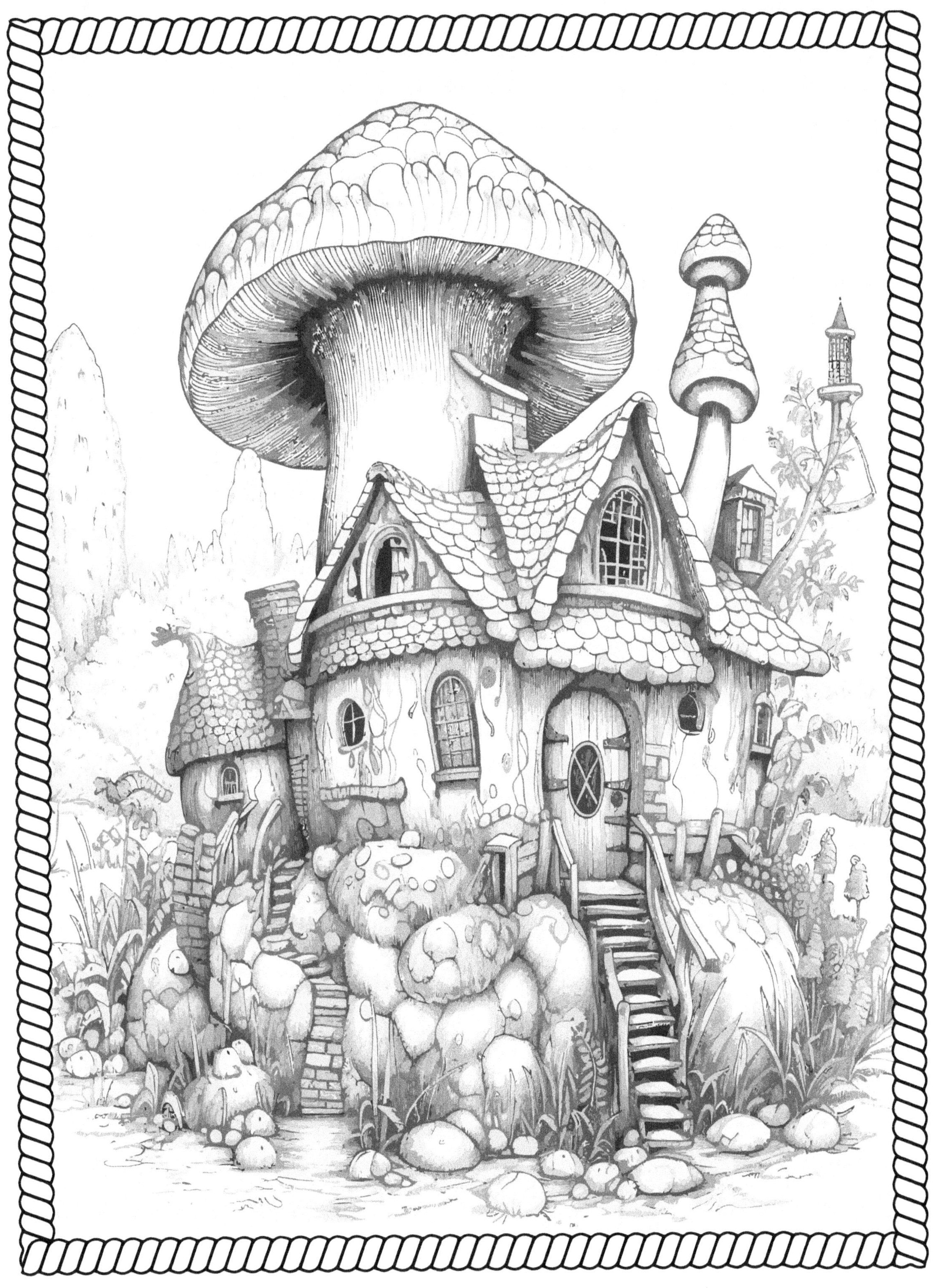

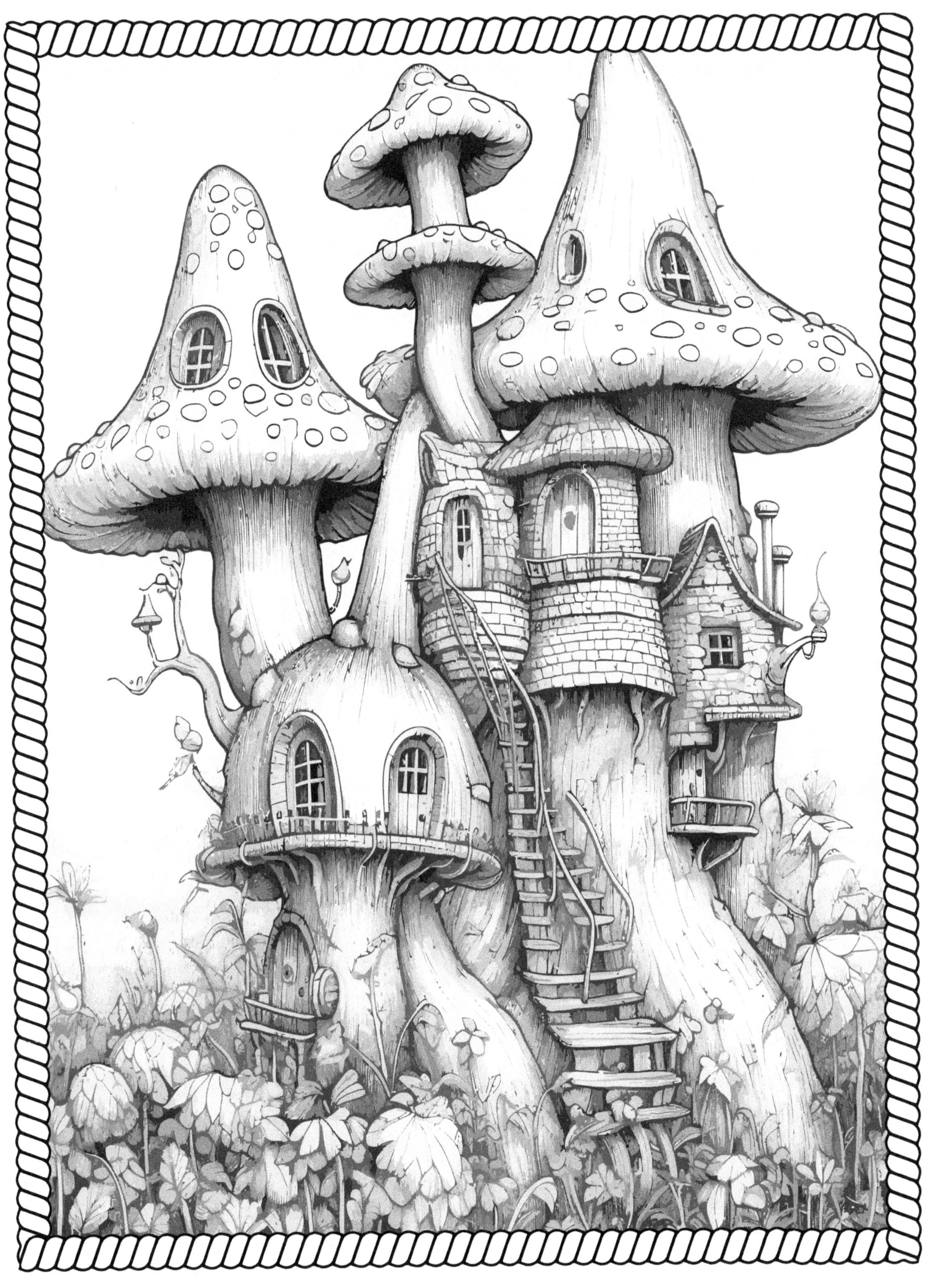

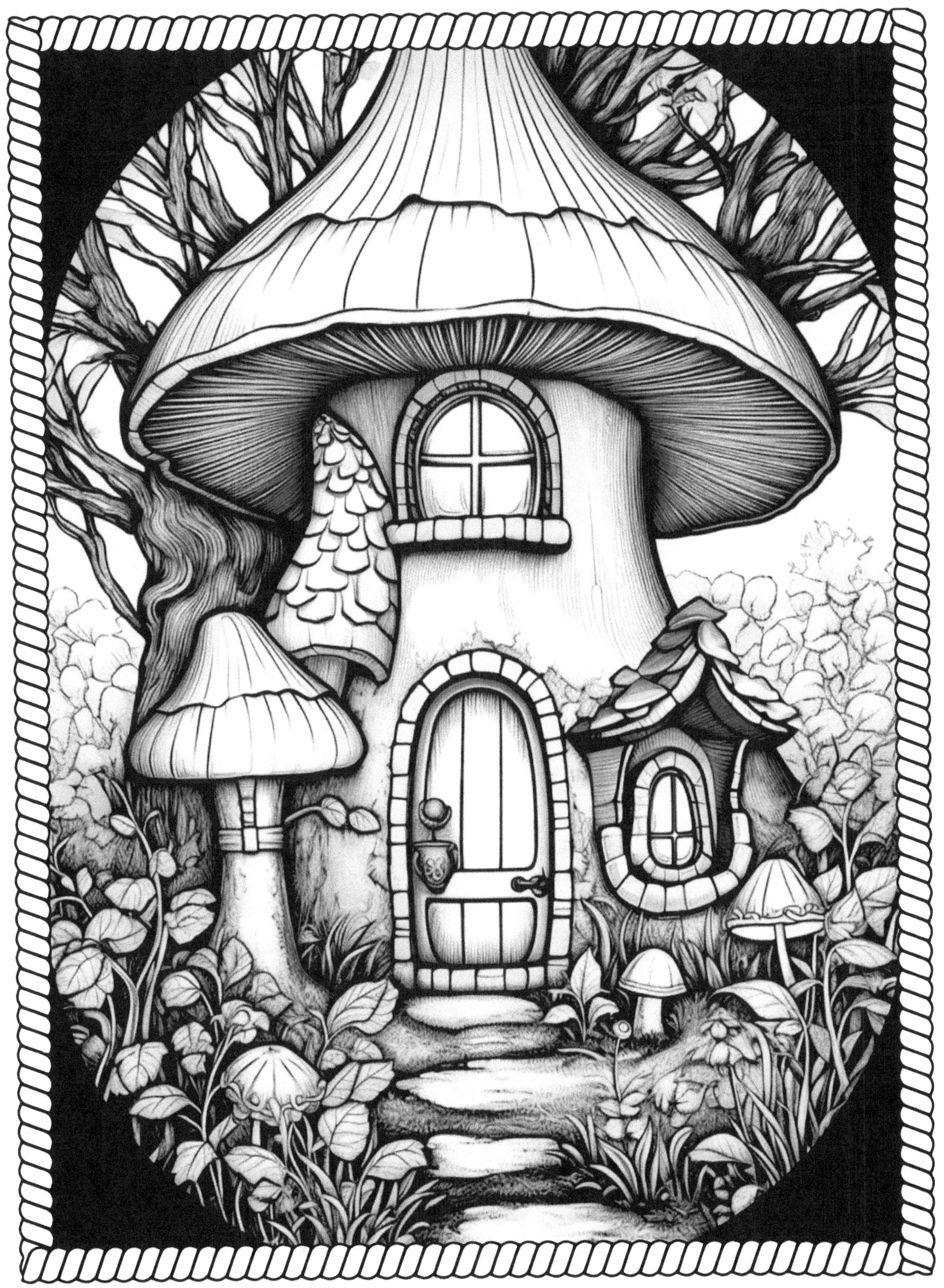

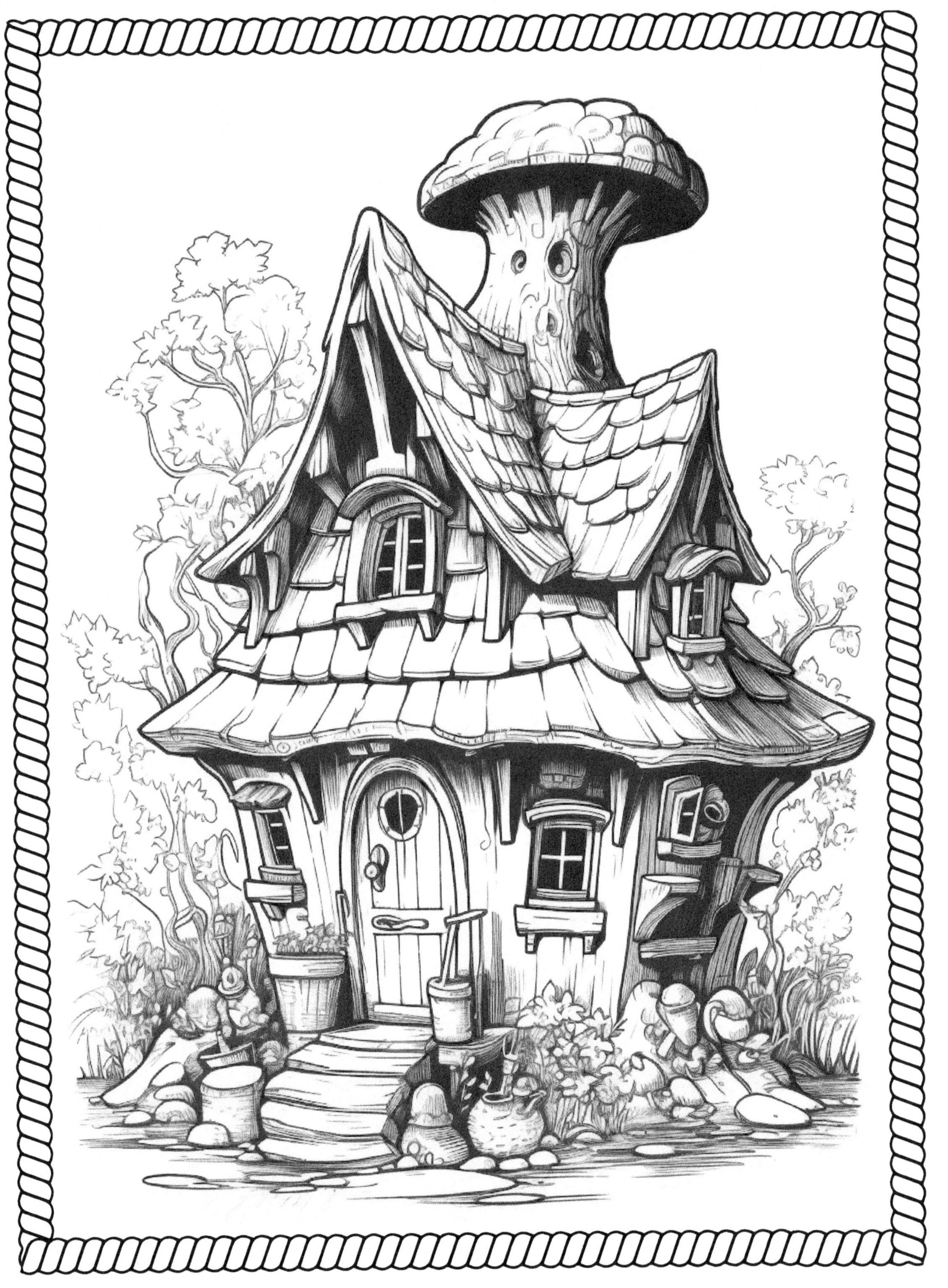

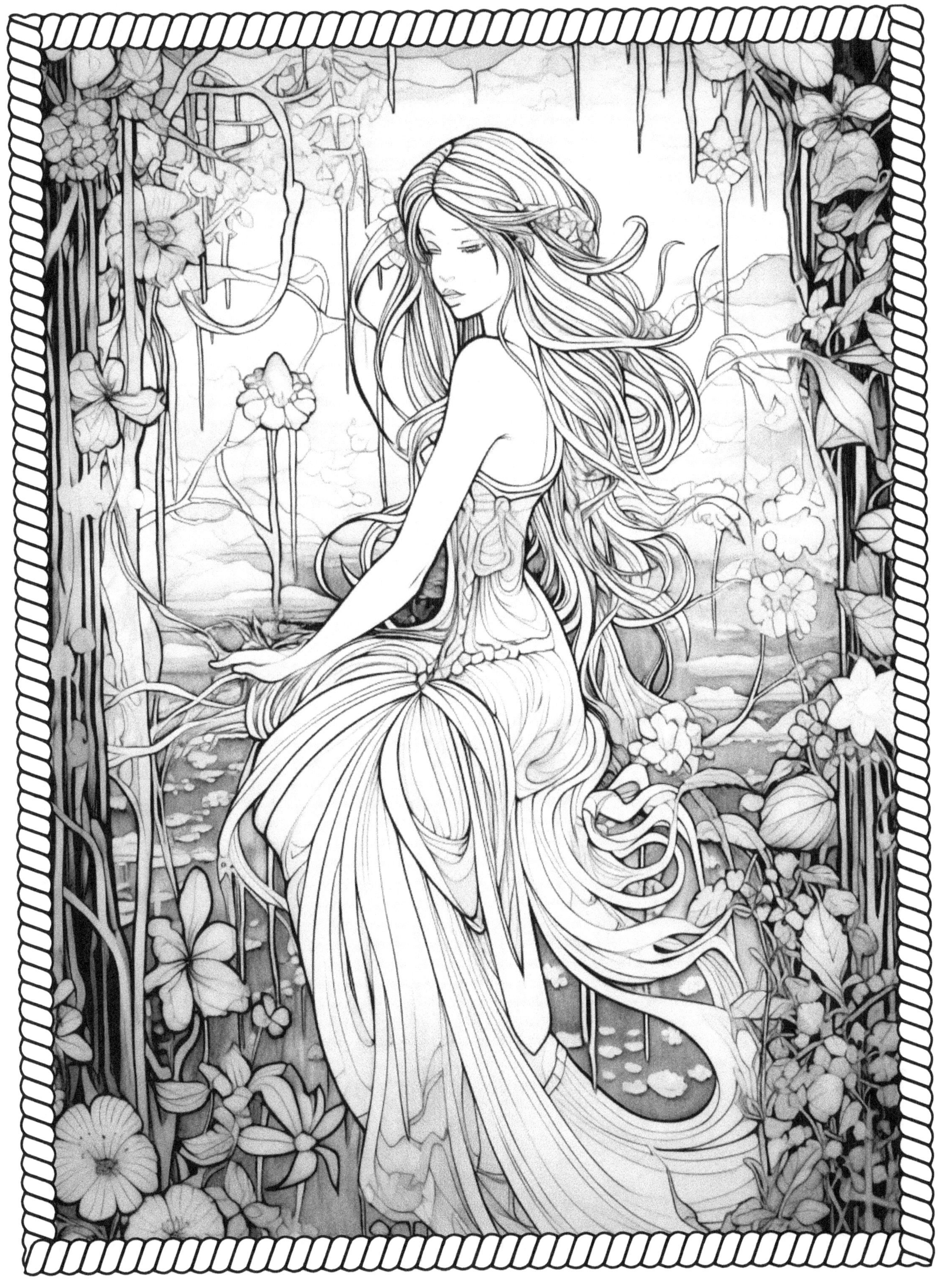

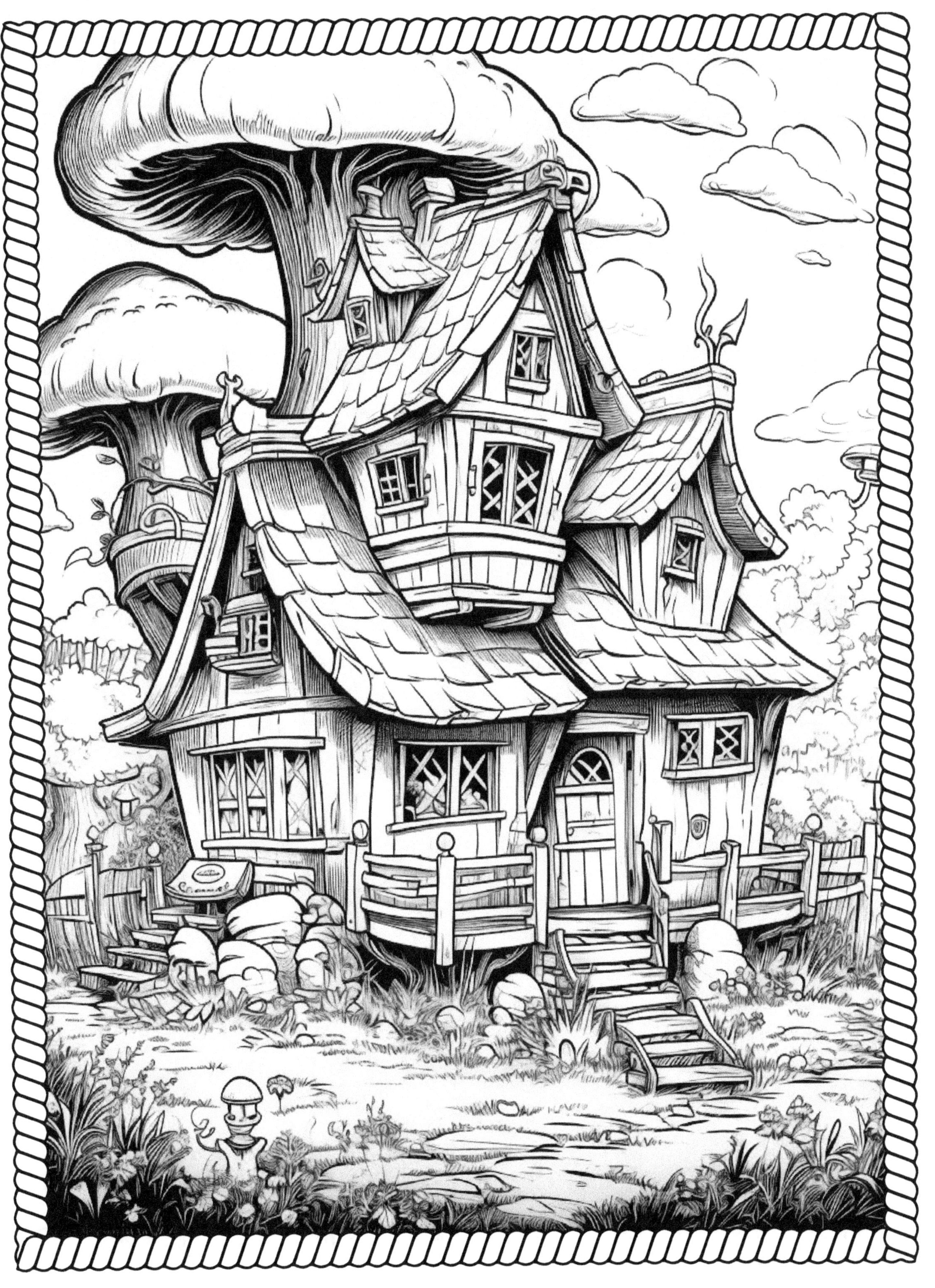

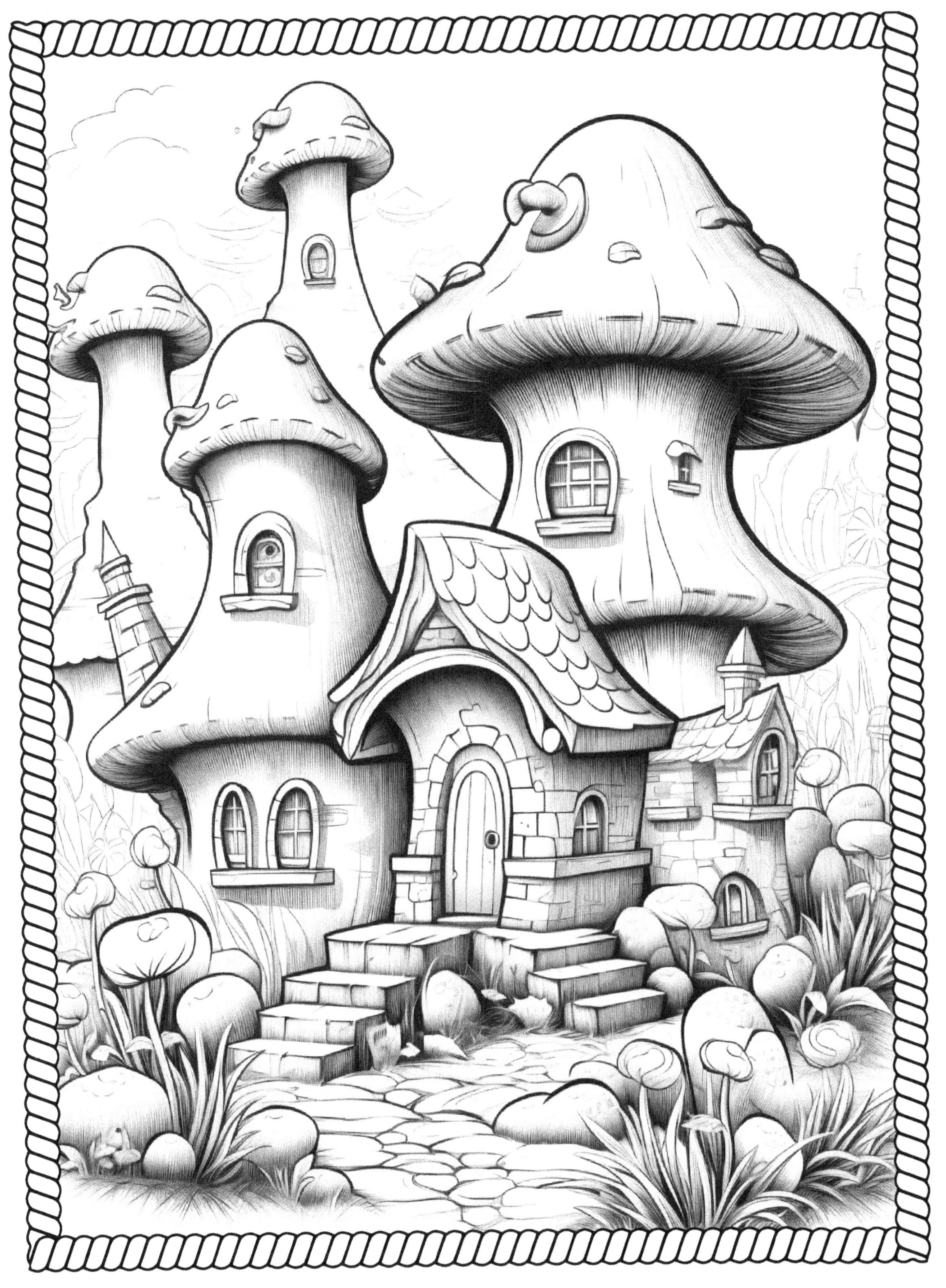